ATTRACTING TOURISTS TO SHOPPING CENTERS

ATTRACTING TOURISTS TO SHOPPING CENTERS

International Council of Shopping Centers
New York

The International Council of Shopping Centers (ICSC) is the trade association of the shopping center industry. Serving the shopping center industry since 1957, ICSC is a not-for-profit organization with over 39,000 members in 77 countries worldwide.

ICSC members include shopping center

- owners
- developers
- managers
- marketing specialists
- leasing agents
- retailers
- researchers
- attorneys

- architects
- contractors
- consultants
- investors
- lenders and brokers
- academics
- public officials

ICSC sponsors more than 300 meetings a year and provides a wide array of services and products for shopping center professionals, including publications and research data.

For more information about ICSC, contact the
International Council of Shopping Centers, 1221 Avenue of the Americas, New York, NY 10020-1099
ICSCNET: www.icsc.org

The International Council of Shopping Centers gratefully acknowledges Mall of America, PIER 39 and Franklin Mills for use of their photographs on the front cover of this book.

This publication is designed to provide accurate and authoritative information in regard to the subject matter covered. It is sold with the understanding that the publisher is not engaged in rendering legal, accounting, or other professional services. If legal advice or other expert assistance is required, the services of a competent professional person should be sought.

—from a Declaration of Principles jointly adopted by a
Committee of the American Bar Association and a
Committee of Publishers.

Published by
International Council of Shopping Centers, New York, NY

Cover Design: Design Plus
Text Design: Stanley S. Drate/Folio Graphics Co. Inc.
ICSC Catalog Number: 184
International Standard Book Number: 1-58268-017-5
Printed in the United States of America

CONTENTS

ACKNOWLEDGMENTS

The International Council of Shopping Centers gratefully acknowledges the following shopping center professionals who contributed their expertise to this book:

Annette Alvarez, CMD
Marketing Director
Dadeland Mall
Miami, Florida

Maureen Cahill
Public Relations Director
Mall of America
Bloomington, Minnesota

Cathy Case, CMD
Associate Director, Marketing
The Rouse Company
Columbia, Maryland

Maureen Taylor Crampton
Marketing Director
The Forum Shops at Caesars
Las Vegas, Nevada

Carolyn J. Feimster, SCMD
President
CJF Marketing International
Hollywood, Florida
Franklin Park, New Jersey

Lydia L. Gilmore, CMD
General Manager
The Shops at Sunset Place
South Miami, Florida

Rose Leone
Director of Tourism
Franklin Mills
Philadelphia, Pennsylvania

Karen MacDonald
Director of Communications
The Taubman Company
Bloomfield Hills, Michigan

Amy Marx
Tourism Manager
Mall of America
Bloomington, Minnesota

Denise M. Rasmussen
Vice President, Travel Sales
PIER 39
San Francisco, California

Ronald Lee Rodriguez
Vice President, Publicity, Special
    Events and Tourism
Burdines—The Florida Store
Miami, Florida

Michele Rothstein
Vice President Marketing
Chelsea GCA Realty, Inc.
Roseland, New Jersey

Robert S. Solomon, SCSM
President
Robert Solomon & Associates LLC
Tarzana, California

Ian F. Thomas
President
Thomas Consultants Inc.
Vancouver, British Columbia

INTRODUCTION

Tourists are an important and growing part of some shopping centers' customer markets. Yet because tourists are travelers from another geographic region or country, a different approach may be needed for them than for a center's core market. *Attracting Tourists to Shopping Centers* provides information on how shopping centers can effectively develop and promote themselves to tourists, whether international travelers or day-trippers from the next city. The book sets out suggestions and practical business strategies on such key topics as how to:

- Develop an effective tourism plan using market research, including ways of carrying out surveys and other research, and putting research findings into practice.
- Work with professionals in the tourism and travel industry.
- Advertise and promote the shopping center to the tourist market in an effective and cost-effective manner.
- Plan special events that appeal to tourists and support the center's overall tourism marketing strategy.
- Create an appealing merchandise mix for tourists.
- Offer amenities that will make the center more tourist-friendly.

Also included are profiles of shopping centers that successfully market to tourists, photographs illustrating aspects of the tourism programs, and a resource list for obtaining further information on this subject.

1

PLANNING TO MARKET TO TOURISTS

Is developing a tourism program an appropriate and worthwhile activity for your shopping center? Before starting a tourism campaign, ask whether your center has the potential to attract a significant tourist market. Are out-of-town travelers and visitors a feasible growth area for your center? If they are, what types of tourists have the greatest potential for you?

Market Research

Consult reports and statistics about tourism in your area collected by local and regional tourist destination organizations. These organizations might include the following:

- Local tourism council
- Chamber of Commerce
- Economic development agency
- Convention and Visitors Bureau (CVB)
- State and regional tourism bureaus.

From these sources and others, look for relevant information, such as:

- Number of visitors to your city or region
- Percentage of that visitor market that shops as part of their trip
- Number of visitors who have shopping potential for your center, such as higher-income tourists for a premium-priced center
- State or city of origin for domestic visitors; home country for international visitors
- Whether other shopping areas in your market appeal to the tourism segment
- Visitor demographics, such as sex, age, nationality, earnings, and so on.

Estimate the current percentage of visitor business in your center. Carry out brief exit surveys of shoppers as they leave the center, asking for the following data:

- The shopper's home country/state/city
- Any purchases made—amount and type.

From these survey contacts, determine:

- Percentage of visitors who are tourists (that is, who live outside the core traffic area)
- Frequency of visits by tourists as a percentage of total shopper visits
- Average tourist spending per visit, in comparison with average visitor spending
- What merchandise or services visitors are purchasing at the center.

Evaluate your center's tourism performance. Using the above information, compare your center's current share of the tourism market with rates of visitation for the area, and ask whether your center is capturing its proportionate share of tourist traffic.

Examine your center's tourist market potential by asking the following questions:

- Is there an opportunity to capture more tourist traffic at your center? Are tourists coming to the area who might include a shopping visit to your center but are not doing so?
- If not, why not? Is business going to the competition instead? What features of your center might account for this? Can these be changed?
- Does your center's potential tourist traffic warrant a special tourist marketing initiative?
- Are there sufficient resources to market to additional tourists and serve them?

Decide whether tourists should be a marketing focus for your center. There is no ready formula for this decision, which depends on the center and the type of shopper involved. Consider the following:

- For some shopping centers, even a small increase in tourist traffic might be considered worthwhile if other sources of shopper traffic are decreasing.
- With a particular high-spending shopper contingent, growth of a few percentage points could represent a significant boost in sales.
- For other centers, however, location or restrictions in merchandise mix may mean there is limited scope for marketing to the visitor.

A center's strategy for marketing to tourists should be based on findings of research about the market. Research is important to:

- Confirm the importance of tourist shopping to the center
- Measure and evaluate the effectiveness of your marketing programs

- Improve future and present marketing efforts
- Demonstrate accountability to the center owners, retailers and managers
- Substantiate budgeting and requests for funding for tourist programs.

Research should focus on the following three areas (see the Market Research Questionnaire on pages 6–7):

- The shopper. Who are your tourist visitors? Secure demographic information such as country or region of origin, age, income and family members.
- The visit to the area. Do tourists visit for business, pleasure or other reasons? Find out what else they do while in town and their preferences in lodging and transportation.
- The visit to the center. Why do tourists visit the center? What sort of purchases are they making? How much do they spend? How do they get to the center, and when?

Centers can use many methods of research to obtain information:

- Conducting periodic exit surveys by questionnaire. This enables selection of visitors who have made a purchase. This may be expensive and time-consuming, but may also produce the most reliable data. Surveying tasks could be contracted out.
- Having visitors fill out information cards to redeem a gift/coupon voucher or other incentive. The cost is minimal but the method may yield less data than a full survey.
- Establishing a Preferred Visitor Program whose application includes information you want to know. An in-mall interactive kiosk system could be used to register shoppers and record information; subsequent visits could also be recorded.
- Ongoing tracking through services offered to visitors. For example, numbers of foreign visitors applying for tax rebates could be noted. Or customer information booth staff could ask for the visitor's country of origin. This is effective when only limited shopper information is sought.
- Surveying tour groups. Group leaders or guides could be asked to furnish details of group demographics when signing in for the visit.
- Conducting exit surveys at the airport to find out your center's share of visitors and their shopping preferences.
- Receiving e-mailed survey forms which the shopper accesses over the center website. Coupons are sent to the respondent in return for this service.

Some further considerations in carrying out research might be these:

- Ideally, surveys should provide information about all shoppers who visit the center—local as well as out-of-town—so that there is a basis for comparison.

Market Research Questionnaire

Customer surveys are customized to a shopping center's marketing objectives, research budget and ability to follow up and use research data. The following parameters could be included in a market research survey of visitors to a shopping center.

Shopper Demographic Information
- Country or region of origin
- First language
- Age
- Gender
- Annual household income
- Marital status
- Number of children
- Profession.

Profile of the Visit to the Area
- Purpose of the visit (such as business, convention, pleasure, family visit, accompanying another person)
- Those accompanying the respondent (such as a spouse, another family member or friends)
- Other local attractions and sites being visited on this trip
- Hours of day/week available for shopping.

Length of Stay

Means of Transportation to the Area
- Own car
- Rental car
- Intercity bus
- Railroad
- Airline
- Tour bus.

Accommodations
- Hotel
- Bed and breakfast
- Home of family or friends
- Other (RV, camping vehicle).

Profile of the Visit to the Center
Is this a repeat or first visit to the center?

For repeat visitors, how long since your last visit to the center?

For first-time visitors, how did you hear about the shopping center?
- Local friends or relatives
- Advertising in newspapers, magazines or other media
- Publicity in newspapers, magazines or other media
- Travel agent(s)
- Airlines
- Travel guidebooks or other travel media
- Tour operators or companies
- Corporate travel department
- Travel destination organizations for the city, state or region
- Personal computer (Internet, e-mail).

Who is the respondent shopping with?
- Business associate(s)
- Friends
- Relatives
- Tour group
- Shopping alone
- School or study group.

Transportation—how did the customer get to the center?
- Tour bus
- Own car
- Rental car
- Limousine or taxi
- Public transportation
- Friend or family.

Shopping Profile
Merchants, restaurants and other retailers and venues visited in the center.

Type of merchandise purchased:
- Gifts/souvenirs
- Food/beverage
- Apparel
- Entertainment
- Electronics
- Other (specify).

Price point of purchases (check one):
- Premium
- Mid-price
- Budget.

Reason for shopping at the center (check one):
- Particular brand names—if so, which ones?
- Selection of merchandise
- Price of merchandise.

Method of payment:
- Credit card
- Cash
- Traveler's checks
- Debit card.

What other local attractions or activities will be included on this outing?

- Data should be benchmarked (so that data can be compared over time) by relating findings for tourists to the average purchase or total mall visits.
- Bilingual (or multilingual) intercept personnel and questionnaires may be required for surveying, so that data are not restricted to English-speakers.
- Sensitivity to cultural scruples and concerns about privacy is crucial in conducting surveys. For example, certain ethnic groups consider salary or earnings levels to be very personal matters, and will tend to respond negatively to requests for information about their income.
- Frequency of surveys will depend in part on the center's funding for research. Twice monthly is common in the industry, but some centers find that surveying every second year provides a reasonable overview of change and growth in their markets.
- Surveying is best carried out at times or seasons when tourists are especially plentiful, to get an accurate cross section of the market. Timing of surveys should take into account seasonal or other factors that could distort findings.
- Coordinating research efforts with your CVB or local tourism board can be efficient and cost-effective.

In marketing to tourists, you will be selling a product—your center—and the overall quality of that product is critical. Does any aspect of your center need improvement to become tourist-friendly and make a favorable impression on out-of-towners? Review and take stock of these and other features:

- Center infrastructure: Is your facility in general good repair and well maintained and cleaned?
- Operations: Does management have an understanding of tourist needs and the resources to extend to a larger tourist market?
- Merchandise mix: Are fresh, new retail concepts and popular retail banners represented?
- Overall mall environment ambience, decor and design: Do these create a welcoming, visually pleasing shopping environment?
- Amenities: Are there adequate guest services, such as an information desk or concierge service, to welcome tourist visitors and orient them to the center? Can the center handle international visitors? Are there parking areas that will accommodate motor coaches? Could service levels be improved?
- Entertainment and dining offerings: Are there sufficient dining and entertainment venues to encourage visitors to spend time in the center and make it the focus of a family outing?
- Strengths and weaknesses: Note the strengths and weaknesses of your center revealed by your research and include them in your tourism marketing plan.

Assess the status and character of tourism in the center in these ways:

- Talk to merchants, asking whether they are seeing significant numbers of tourist shoppers and the estimated contribution of tourist spending to sales.
- Ask personnel at the information booth, concierge station and other service areas about frequency of tourist visits, and what kinds of tourists they have observed most frequently.
- Walk the center to observe the level of activity at visitor-oriented areas such as the information booth or souvenir kiosk.

Ask the opinions of a variety of shoppers and people involved with retailing and/or tourism:

- Poll shoppers either formally or informally to ask what they like and dislike about the center.
- Invite tourism council representatives and members of the hospitality industry (such as hotel managers, bus drivers or managers of visitor attractions) to tour the center and rate its tourism potential. Survey forms might be used to record their reactions.
- Establish a tourism advisory board that includes members of the tourism professions.
- Ask employees about aspects of the center that need improvement.

Utilizing Research Findings

Create a tourism marketing plan and budget as a separate extension of the center's overall marketing plan. This process should include the following four steps:

- Analyze the center's strengths and weaknesses.
- Compare the center's strengths and weaknesses with those of the competition.
- Identify goals and objectives for your marketing.
- Develop strategies and tactics with a realistic budget and flexible timetable.

Particular findings from the research can be used in developing specific aspects of your tourism marketing plan. For example, the number of tourist visits to the center and volume of visits as a percentage of total shopper visits can help you:

- Establish relative importance of tourists to the center's total market.
- Decide how to allot marketing resources.
- Determine whether tourist activity has changed since the last survey, and if so, how.
- Identify the tourist segment that has the greatest potential to deliver

Tourist Profiles

Market research can provide important information about the tourists visiting your center. Broad general knowledge about your center's target market or markets, however, can be equally important. Extend your understanding of the market through different avenues, such as these:

- Personal contact. Become acquainted with tourist shoppers by talking with them personally, observing them and getting to know their values and expectations in shopping. What aspects of the center and its merchandise are most important to your tourist profile groups—brand merchandise and prices, or a leisurely visit to the center with browsing and dining? For center management staff who may not have direct contact with many shoppers, regular feedback from customer service booth personnel or customer service staff in retail stores may provide similar information.

- Cultural understanding. Try to understand the frame of mind of important traveler groups; talk with them, read about the culture of international visitors. Learn about the habits and travel patterns of key tourist visitor groups. Europeans enjoy extensive summer vacations, for example, which may be important times for visits. Senior citizens may travel frequently to other localities for January retail sales.

- A global view. Evaluate industry trends in both tourism and shopping by reading economic reports, newspapers and local business and trade publications. Read magazines and newsletters for the travel industry targeting the countries that your tourists come from, such as Latin America's newsmagazines for travel agents. Keep track of world news affecting your feeder markets. Financial media and e-mail news services can point up pertinent world trends that affect shopping, such as national currency devaluations or economic news.

sales—i.e., day-trippers, conventioneers, business travelers, domestic, international, and so on.

Alternatively, data about the timing and frequency of tourist visits to the center could help determine whether the center's peak visitor periods correspond to the area's peak visitor periods. Data about how visitors traveled to the locality can determine appropriate media for advertising and promotion—for example, billboards at airport facilities might be useful if most visitors have traveled to the locality by air.

Data about tourists' accommodations could:

- Determine lodgings that are good potential marketing partners.
- Help assess importance of the VFR ("visiting friends and relatives") factor for tourists coming to the center, and the need to market to local residents.

Information secured from visits to other area attractions or businesses could be useful in identifying which businesses and attractions could co-market to tourists or become venues for center advertisements. Data about how the tourist heard about the center could help in selection of effective advertising vehicles or media. Personal data about visitors, including name, street and e-mail addresses, and phone and fax numbers, could be used for direct marketing by mail or telephone.

Information about visitors' country of origin could help to:

- Identify important potential visitor groups. Using profiling, decide which types of tourists are most likely to patronize the center.
- Target advertising to feeder (home) markets of tourists.
- Advise retailers about addressing special needs of visitors, such as offering tailoring or alterations for differently proportioned groups, or stocking smaller-sized clothing inventory for Asian shoppers.

Information on tourists' native languages could indicate the need to translate mall literature and press kits, or to hire bilingual or multilingual staff.

Market research findings can be an important tool for negotiating with other parties who have an interest in your center's marketing. Following are a few ways to effectively utilize this information:

- Use analyses of research to win support from center ownership for funding of tourism marketing, and/or to sell a particular marketing initiative.
- Communicate important findings to managers and staff of the center and of retail stores, to encourage them to focus on marketing to tourists.
- Share results with retailers at the center, so that they can become aware of the need to market their own stores with the tourist market in mind.
- Refer to research statistics in discussion with marketing partners, to demonstrate results of marketing for negotiating purposes.

- Share data with your local CVB, travel agents and tourism agencies as part of mutual pooling of information and to gain credibility as a tourism collaborator.

Evaluating Your Plan

Once a tourist marketing strategy has been put into practice, regular market research can provide an objective means of measuring the success of your total tourism program and its parts. Use research to assess the efficacy and cost-effectiveness of your marketing efforts, and to prioritize and budget for different tourism programs. Some of the many indicators are:

- Comparison of spending by all tourists in the center with the cost of marketing and operating of special tourist programs.
- Productivity assessment of different tourist profiles or groups, such as travelers from a certain country; compare average per-person purchases for the group with average tourist sales to identify the most profitable tourists.

2

WORKING WITH THE VISITOR INDUSTRY

A shopping center can develop a tourism campaign more effectively by partnering with other agencies and professionals in the travel and tourism industry. These may include:

- Travel and tourism groups:

  - Activity and event coordinators
  - Convention organizers
  - Travel agents
  - Tour operators
  - Human resources or travel coordinators at educational institutions and major corporations
  - Tourism industry associations.

- The lodgings industry:

  - Hotels
  - Hostels
  - Bed and breakfasts.

- Transportation companies:

  - Airlines
  - Limousine and taxicab drivers
  - Transportation terminals and airports
  - Car rental agencies
  - Motor coach operators.

- Community and government agencies:

  - Tourism council
  - Chamber of Commerce
  - Convention and Visitors Bureau (CVB)
  - Economic development authority
  - Regional and state tourism agencies.

Networking and collaborating with these professionals offer the following advantages:

- Greater access to information about tourists in your area and their activities.
- Pooling of resources, ideas and expertise.
- Extended scope and a broader audience for advertising and other marketing campaigns.
- Savings in time and expense for visitor marketing programs.

The Partnering Relationship

Many types of collaborative relationships are possible within the travel sector, such as:

- Teaming up for marketing purposes.
- Developing travel packages—many shopping centers join with travel organizers, hotels and transportation companies to offer inclusive travel packages with discounted accommodation and airfare or other benefits and visits to a shopping mall.
- Co-sponsoring special events.

Before approaching other tourist industry professionals, be ready to work constructively with them.

- Identify organizations, agencies and businesses that are appropriate and potentially advantageous to work with (see list above).
- Appoint a designated liaison for marketing to tourists, so that travel professionals and media can readily approach your center on visitor-related matters. A tourism telephone extension can also direct inquiries from these individuals.
- Prepare high-quality publicity materials, such as a comprehensive press kit about your center. Depending on your intended marketing scope, specialized materials for certain groups may be needed, such as translated versions in other languages.
- Create an itinerary and accompanying talk for tours of the shopping center.

Working relationships with representatives of the visitor industry will be useful now and in the long term. Initiate contacts with a one-on-one approach:

- Talk individually to travel or tour organizers at a travel show, and follow up with a call or letter afterward.
- Make first contacts with prospective local partners at the grassroots level—ask for an appointment with the local hotel manager, for example, "to discuss how we can work together to attract more tourists."

Present a specific proposal for cooperatively marketing together.

- Describe a specific action plan with specific results.

- Demonstrate the benefits or advantages of your suggestions to your potential partner.
- Stipulate what each party will contribute. The center might provide publicity, incentives such as coupon vouchers or gifts, or transportation to the center, among other possibilities.
- Be involved in developing any joint package and publicity materials in order to maintain control of the way in which the center and its image are presented.

Acquaint potential partners with your center. Following your one-on-one introduction, invite members of the media and travel professions such as tour operators and travel agents for a special tour of the center. Components of the tour might include:

- Explanation of the center's merchandise offerings, its facilities and any special services that are available for tourists
- Introduction to the center's tourism director or other designated staff liaison personnel
- Refreshments or a meal for attendees, and/or coupon books and a souvenir of the center (baseball cap, shopping bag, T-shirt, etc.)
- Handouts in the form of press kits, center directories and maps, press releases on upcoming events, and the tourism director's business card.

Join key industry trade organizations such as TIA (Travel Industry Association of America), NTA (National Tour Association), the concierge association or the regional travel associations serving the center's tourist feeder areas.

Cultivate relationships by offering hospitality and expressing appreciation. Host parties or other functions periodically for travel industry representatives to thank those who have referred business to the center. Besides offering refreshments and entertainment, you might hand out prizes to those who have made the most referrals, or referrals of greatest value.

Tap into the power of friendly personal relations. Generally, people are most willing to work with someone they like. An enthusiastic, dedicated staff member(s) should serve as ongoing contact person with visitor-related businesses and agencies, cultivating and maintaining relationships with important partners and contacts. Consistency and continuity—having the same liaison person on hand—are valuable in fostering cooperative relationships on a long-term basis.

Travel and Tourism Groups

Tour operators, travel agencies and convention planners are increasingly aware of the importance of shopping in tourist visits. Among the ways to initiate an alliance are the following:

- Approach local travel agencies, travel brokers and convention or tour organizers to suggest working together.

Getting More Mileage From Trade Shows

Conventions and trade shows of the travel and tourism industry are important opportunities for establishing contacts and marketing your center. The following steps may be helpful in obtaining maximum benefits from these events.

Have a game plan:
- Before the show, obtain a list of agencies and operators who will attend, and identify those which are most relevant to your center's tourist market.
- Make appointments with and write an introductory letter to those whom you plan to see in person.
- Have goals for your contacts, and use appointment time efficiently by
  - Being ready with information about the center.
  - Having a proposal or plan for co-promoting.
  - Providing something for the contact to take away in the form of brochures, press releases, a center T-shirt or shopping bag, photos of the mall—be sure that handouts include a contact person's name, phone and address.

Use pre- and post-show opportunities:
- Allow extra time before and after the show to make additional contacts with attending travel professionals.
- If the trade show is in a key feeder market, use the visit as an opportunity to market to consumers, media and travel agents in that area. Host a dinner or fashion show for travel professionals as well as influential social and community leaders.

Have high visual impact:
- Stand out with a highly visible booth at the show. Materials such as shopping bags from different mall merchants are colorful props.
- Show as well as tell what your center is like. Use pictures and photos in your presentation area and your literature that reinforce the image of the center you want to project. Include photos in handouts as an aid to remembering your center.

Maintain personal contact:
- Attend a show in person if possible. Contracting out representation at travel trade functions is an alternative, but it fails to forge any permanent relationship with contacts.
- Follow up personally with a note or call to contacts after returning from the convention. Keep contacts' names and addresses handy for future shows.

- Make contact with out-of-town travel professionals who market the center's area as a travel destination by attending trade shows of the travel industry (TIA, World Travel Market, London). Depending on the center's tourist profiles and marketing budget, it may be worthwhile to attend major shows abroad in those countries from which many of the center's tourist visitors come. (See Getting More Mileage from Trade Shows, on page 18.)

Specific marketing strategies to use in partnership with these professionals might include the following:

- The center provides special discount coupons for tour participants; the travel agent, convention planner or tour organizer includes the coupons in the tour or convention package.
- Airline ticket wholesalers and travel agencies distribute center marketing packets (such as discount coupons) with travel documents—for example, including center discount coupons when mailing tickets and itinerary to a client. This gets information about the center to travelers before they leave home, enabling them to include the center in their trip planning.
- The shopping center offers familiarization ("fam") tours of the center to appropriate tour or convention groups. Demand is often for tours with a retailing or business-oriented focus, describing the management and workings of the center. Time for shopping after the tour is included in the visit itinerary.
- The mall and/or its retailers could offer events for spouses or families of convention attendees. For a successful program:

  - Assess potential attendance from a particular convention by asking the convention hotel whether a high proportion of rooms booked are double rooms—a reliable indicator that conventioneers are traveling with other family members.
  - Team up with a local children-friendly attraction to offer a children's outing. Include promotions such as discounted movie passes to a cinema in the mall.
  - Base spouse programs around subjects that tie in with the center's stores, such as fashion shows or cooking demonstrations.

The Lodgings Industry

Hotels offer many possibilities for co-marketing. Identify potential partners by looking for hotels in your area whose guests match your shopper profile. Hotels should be appropriate in price point—a budget hotel is not a good prospect if most shoppers at your center are drawn from the upper-income range. A hotel located in or adjacent to the mall should have strong potential. Hotels that do not have their own retail stores are likely to be most responsive.

Lake Buena Vista Caters to Hospitality Workers

Lake Buena Vista Factory Stores in Orlando can be compared to a bobcat in the same big cage with a mighty lion. But the little bobcat is roaring to be heard in a market that is the world's No. 1 tourist destination.

The big lion is Belz Enterprises, which operates more than 900,000 sf of outlet space in three centers on International Drive not far from the Venture Outlet Centers' 170,000-sf Lake Buena Vista Factory Stores. The 720,000-sf Belz Outlet World (composed of Malls 1 and 2 and an annex) is Orlando's second most popular attraction, behind Disney World.

Despite the competition, two-year-old Lake Buena Vista is grabbing its slice of the big Orlando pie by racking up comp sales increases of 20 to 25 percent due to an aggressive marketing program, says marketing director Leigh Jones.

To reach the estimated 47 million tourists and convention goers that annually visit the Orlando area, the Lake Buena Vista center, only two miles from a main entrance to Disney World, has launched an in-depth Hospitality Referral Program. According to Jones, the way to tourists' hearts is through the area's 80,000 hospitality industry employees.

In this program, Lake Buena Vista distributes vouchers to concierges, bellhops, bus drivers, theme park employees and other people in the hospitality industry, who sign or mark the vouchers with their company or personal names and then hand them out to their customers. Customers can then turn in the vouchers at the outlet center for $300 worth of percentage-off coupons.

Jones says the most successful month so far in the program was February, when 1,324 vouchers were turned in.

The coupon packs also are available on the center's Web site.

Back to the 80,000 employees: The center gives them various incentives to hand out the vouchers, including a thank-you party. In June, 1,600 hospitality industry workers whose names appeared on vouchers were honored. The evening event, held at the center, featured free food, entertainment and door prizes.

The biggest prize, one year's free use of a Jeep, went to Jeff Pilarski, owner of First Class Tours, a vacation rental service in Orlando. A light rain didn't spoil the evening, nor did smoke visible in the distance from one of the numerous summer forest fires in Florida.

Co-sponsors of the event were Universal Studios, *Where* magazine and the Florida Hospitality Industry Association.

—By Donald Finley
from *Value Retail News*
September 1998

Approach hotel management to suggest marketing the center to guests. Specific marketing approaches might include:

- Displaying shopping center materials in brochure racks in the lobby and placing visitors' books or information packages in guest rooms.
- Marketing to participants in upcoming conferences or other group meetings who stay at the hotel. A concierge might assist with distribution of center information in the lobby, in guest rooms or in convention packages.
- Offering discount benefits to each other's customers. Shoppers could receive a special shopping bag with coupons from the shopping center information desk on presentation of a hotel key. The hotel in turn could offer discounts to their guests who shop at the center, with a cashier's slip or other proof of purchase from a merchant at the center entitling the shopper to a discounted room rate.
- Joining together with area hotels, motels and restaurants or other local businesses to create shopping packages. Examples:

  - The hotel might offer a discounted room rate and special perks such as free use of the fitness center; participating restaurants might offer a complimentary "shopper's power breakfast" and the shopping center would provide logoed shopping bags with coupon books and mall directories. Additional services such as free transportation from the hotel to the mall could also be included. Marketing of packages is usually the responsibility of the hotel.
  - Shopping packages can be based around weekends, holiday periods or primary shopping seasons such as late November to develop a time frame and theme.

- Working through the concierges at larger local hotels. They have personal contact with individual visitors and can:

  - Provide information about upcoming visitor groups.
  - Distribute shopping center maps or information to tourists.
  - Refer hotel guests to the center.

- Organizing a shuttle van or limo service from hotel to center. The hotel often covers the expense of such a service, but individual arrangements vary.

Cultivate relationships with hotel personnel by:

- Keeping management and concierges updated on arrivals of new merchandise that has an appropriate price point for their guests
- Reminding them of amenities for visitors that are available at the mall, such as bilingual store personnel
- Providing suggested shopping lists for visitor groups. A mall could fur-

nish a directory of selected merchandise items offered by its stores, which would make appropriate gifts for business contacts

- Raising awareness of the center with professional concierge associations in your market area—they are usually organized regionally within each state
- Providing function space at your center as an extension of the hotel's facilities.

Transportation Companies

Partnership arrangements can be set up between your shopping center and airlines serving your community. Together, the center and airline could:

- Distribute special gifts to airline passengers who shop at your center (upon presentation of an airline ticket). Gifts could be varied to reflect the amount of the visitor's purchases in the center.
- Offer shopping-themed travel packages, including airline fare with coupons or other incentives provided by the mall. Shuttle service, a discounted hotel room rate, meals or other features could be rolled into such packages.
- Provide stopover packages allowing full-fare passengers passing through the shopping center's area to stay for a set period (usually up to forty-eight hours) with no fare penalty, with shopping as a suggested activity. Mall gifts or coupon packages could be provided to participants.
- Arrange to allow redemption of "frequent flyer" points for dollar-specific certificates good for merchandise at the shopping center.
- Discount day-trip return fares with the shopping center as the destination.

Among local transportation companies to consider approaching as partners are the following:

- Train, limousine, helicopter, trolley or bus services in your center's area. Develop packages or discount offers combining a shopping visit with transportation to and from the center.
- Car rental companies. Develop a special rate with the rental company and promote it through coupons that are redeemable at the center.

Other Partnerships

When seeking partners, explore regional, national and international possibilities in addition to local ones. Recommendations:

- Work with the state tourism office or the federal Department of Commerce, if appropriate.

- Join and/or participate in the conferences of travel trade organizations such as the TIA PowWow and American Bus Association (ABA) annual convention.
- Investigate membership or partnership with trade associations that are involved in tourism from other countries.

Community and Government Agencies

The local tourism council or other non-affiliated agency can be a resource and partner in a shopping center's tourism programs. Suggestions to consider:

- Solicit information from the agency about the visitors coming to the area and the dates of local conventions, sports and cultural events that bring visitors to the area.
- Request that the shopping center be included as a tourist attraction in the agency's media releases, publicity materials, videos and presentations, promotional literature and advertisements. Ask to have the center's publicity materials and coupon packets displayed and distributed in the agency's offices and information centers, since your shopping center adds an element—shopping—to the city or state package for the tourism industry.
- Investigate the possibility of establishing an official tourist information center in the shopping center. Offices of local tourism agencies and satellites of regional and state tourism groups are frequently located in shopping malls. Such a center can help to attract tourist traffic, and travelers who stop to pick up maps or brochures may stay to browse or make a purchase. The shopping center will benefit from the highway directional signage typically installed to alert motorists to the tourism center. A tourist center could be as simple as an information brochure rack at the customer service counter; or on a larger scale, it might be a store with full signage, its own staff and an extensive selection of materials. Costs of a tourism satellite are typically borne by the tourist office.
- Support events that are sponsored by the tourism agency. Participate in its meetings or conventions, join in the local seasonal festivals or other community occasions, and make financial contributions to campaigns that relate to tourism.
- Offer to promote local attractions and events in the shopping center. A center might publicize a tourism fair on murals painted on unused walls in the mall, with expenses shared by the tourism council or other sponsors of special events. In return, those sponsors could carry advertisements for the shopping center in their newsletters, publicity materials and radio ads. Publicize the murals with media coverage and a launch party or breakfast for members of the travel and tourism council.

- Participate in appropriate trade missions or other delegations sponsored by the tourism or economic development authorities. Many states, regions and cities actively seek recognition and liaison with overseas locales by sending a delegation of representatives from important business, educational and cultural interests in the community. Shopping centers and leading retailers are increasingly represented on such tours, for which they typically pay their own expenses.
- Propose cooperative marketing programs involving other local parties. The tourism office or other agency can package the center with museums and other local attractions as a destination in its literature and promotions. Or it could partner with local hotels, restaurants and the shopping center to produce a visitor-oriented campaign or brochure. Competing shopping centers can be brought together under the aegis of the tourism office to co-produce a shopping brochure or map for tourists.

Evaluate Your Partnerships

Keep track of the referrals the center receives from different marketing collaborators, so that you know which ones are bringing the most business to the center. This might be done in one or more of the following ways:

- Use vouchers that are stamped or otherwise marked differently for each hotel, tourist office or other partner; then keep weekly or monthly counts of how many are redeemed from each.
- If the center has its own shuttle service, have the driver record the number of guests who arrive from each hotel on a daily basis; then track these.
- Monitor how many participants attend your center's programs for conventioneers, and compare with the total number of attendees, to see if referrals from the convention organizer or hotel have been strong.

If referrals from a particular hotel or partner are found to be slipping, either discontinue that relationship or work to encourage closer ties.

3

Advertising

From research and shopper surveys, identify the features and qualities that attract out-of-area visitors to the center. Depending on the center, these could include:

- A scenic or very convenient location
- A particular selection of retailers (such as value-price outlets) or a large selection of stores
- An attractive mall environment—a place to relax and browse
- Unique stores and retailers with fashionable brand names
- Entertainment venues and restaurants
- Shopping without taxes or duties
- Family amusement and recreation facilities.

Develop an identity or theme for the center "brand" that includes these high-appeal features, and use it consistently in all advertising. In developing a brand for the center, it may be necessary to decide whether to position the center primarily as a retail or as an entertainment destination. If the center has a strong entertainment component such as an in-mall amusement park, this will need to be advertised separately as a primary destination. Shopping then becomes secondary in your ads.

Positioning

Position and package the shopping center as an attraction, not just a shopping venue. This can be done in many ways:

- Present the center as a destination—a place to spend time and to be entertained. Provide information about restaurants, amusements and entertainment features at the mall.

- Stress a sense of place—the uniqueness of your culture or locale—in mall decor and marketing, such as the exotic scenery of the islands in a Hawaiian center.
- Have a strong visual component in advertising vehicles to convey excitement and appeal.
- Mention nearby tourist attractions for both individuals and families ("Just two miles from Fun Village") to encourage families or groups to include the mall in an excursion.

Maximize Ads

Below are some suggested rules of thumb for maximizing advertisement results per dollar:

- Track all ads to determine how visitors are responding to your center's media campaigns. Capitalize on the ones that yield the highest response.
- Be selective in your target markets. Centers may prefer to focus advertising on higher-spending tour groups or tourist profiles for best sales results.
- Assess the quality of the media you choose, asking to what extent your advertising message is actually communicated to the tourist. This might involve:
  - Checking audited circulation figures for print media.
  - Checking actual distribution of "freebie" publications that are distributed at no cost to the recipient. Are such materials circulated in locations where you want to reach tourists, and are they prominently displayed?
  - Investigating actual readership of free-circulation print media. Ask concierges, the tourist bureau or other sources to see if they observe tourists consulting these publications.

The Tourism Industry

Travel professionals such as travel wholesalers, tour operators and travel agents can publicize the center to many potential tourist shoppers as well as to colleagues in the travel industry, bringing greater returns than might be gotten by marketing directly to the tourist. They also spread the message in the planning stages of the trip, so that it can be included as a stop in a tour itinerary.

Feeder Markets

Advertise to tourists in their home markets, before they travel to your area. Many travelers decide on an itinerary (including where they will shop) before departing for their destination, so early advertising works best. Use the Internet, connections with travel agents and well-timed ad campaigns to reach the tourist in the decision-making phase.

Building prearrival awareness of the center also means that the advertising message is reinforced when tourists are exposed to your center ads after arriving in your region; such double exposure increases the likelihood of a visit.

Representatives of the Media

Media awareness of your center and its features can lead to additional—sometimes free—coverage. To cultivate media attention, you can:

- Provide updated press releases and photographs at regular intervals.
- Furnish pertinent information about special events or new center features.
- Hold "fam" tours, promotional campaign launches or other parties for news media and travel writers.
- Look for ways to partner with media, such as swapping editorial coverage for purchase of a media ad.

Partnerships

Tap into the collaborative relationships your center has established to gain extra mileage for center advertising. The local CVB or bank or other business might participate in a joint advertising campaign or contribute financially to a center's ad campaign in exchange for inclusion of its logo.

Category-Specific Advertising

Marketing to tourists will usually require development of a separate ad campaign or at least a modification of your center's local-market advertisements for the tourist market. (You can save some costs if your tourist advertising is adapted from your local-market ads.) It will also involve marketing to travel industry professionals such as tour operators or travel agents. Be aware of your target market when designing ads.

Ads for Tourist Groups

Advertisements should consider the different shopping priorities of various tourist groups. Shopping centers find that certain types of shoppers have different purchasing profiles:

- Day-trippers such as those on bus tours are more likely to seek out bargains, while overnight visitors tend to be more impulsive in their shopping.
- "High season" arrivals are typically first-time visitors to your area and your center. They are usually more interested in gifts and souvenirs and may be less experienced travelers. They are heavily influenced by pre-trip planning and by information gathered before leaving home.
- "Low season" arrivals are more likely to be repeat visitors to the area and often to your center. They are generally more interested in buying things for themselves and are likely to be bargain hunters. They are more experienced travelers and will react to information they receive after arrival.

Ads for the Travel and Tourism Industry

Members of the travel and tourism industry such as tour operators, motor-coach companies or travel brokers have different information needs than the traveler because they are planning all-inclusive itineraries, often for large groups. In advertising to this professional market, shopping centers should provide details about:

- The center's retail offerings—number of stores, price point(s), retailers' names, places to eat, and features that might appeal to particular groups such as seniors or students
- Services or special programs for tourists, such as group shopping discounts, special events, "fam" tours and availability of interpreters
- Amenities or benefits for the driver, tour organizer or leader, such as a coupon book, a lounge, free refreshments or meals
- Practical considerations for including the center in a broader tour—such as information about nearby attractions and accommodations, and a map of the area and the center's location.

When to Advertise

A tourist's opportunities to come to your center are limited, so timing of ads is critical. Some points to consider in scheduling advertising are:

- Seasonality. Tourist visits may be concentrated at certain times of year. Generally, the most effective advertising reaches the tourist prior to a trip. This means planning ad campaigns well before the peak tourist seasons.
- Frequency. Advertisements must be repeated often to have an impact on their audience. Even then, the results of advertising do not develop in the short term—the real effects of any ad campaign take considerable time to be realized.

Where to Advertise

There are many potentially effective media options for advertising to tourists who have arrived in the center's local area. Among them are:

- Print media:

  - Local and regional daily and weekly newspapers
  - Official visitors' guides, tourist office or Chamber of Commerce maps of the area
  - Hotel in-room directories, broadsheet guides to local events, complimentary visitors' guidebooks and newspapers
  - Special supplements in newspapers
  - Travel-related consumer periodicals (in-flight magazines, newspaper and magazine travel sections and supplements).

- Broadcast media:

  - Local radio and television stations
  - Closed-circuit television in hotel rooms and other venues such as airports and airline in-flight videos.

- Other effective advertising vehicles:

  - Outdoor billboards and signage in public places frequented by tourists, from transportation terminals, such as airport lounge and waiting areas, to street and highway sidings
  - Visitor books placed in hotel rooms
  - Exterior and interior posters in buses, subway cars, shuttle buses
  - Hotel key cards with printed ads on them giving information, inviting guests to visit, present their key and receive a special offer
  - Brochures and cards placed in racks at local tourism offices, hotels, theaters, historic and cultural attractions, transportation hubs, convention sites, car rental agencies, local restaurants, and so on
  - Rental car ad cards that hang from the rearview mirror
  - Coupons given to all deplaning passengers—this requires cooperation of the airline(s)
  - Free directories of the center distributed to hotels and taxi and limo drivers.

Advertising in the tourists' home market can be highly effective. Among the advertising options in feeder markets are:

- Consumer media:

  - Newspaper travel supplements and regular travel sections; general interest, travel and leisure magazines that match your shopper profiles
  - For foreign visitors, use travel guides to your state or area that are circulated in the target country
  - Local radio and television stations can be effective for targeting a specific domestic city or region.

Tourism Sales Promotion

MEADOWOOD MALL
RENO, NEV.

Meadowood Mall saw huge sales potential in the 4.7 million tourists that visit its market each year. Surveys had shown that tourists spent $82 per trip on shopping and that 84% of visitors to the area intended to return. Therefore, Meadowood directed its marketing efforts at getting more visitors into the mall more often.

Objectives

1. To coordinate a comprehensive, cost-effective advertising plan, targeted to visitors, that highlights Meadowood's unique retail offerings. 2. To attract tourists to Meadowood with programs and services not available at the competition. 3. To continue expanding programs targeted to convention attendees. 4. To increase traffic and sales from large visitor groups.

Implementation

Meadowood designed its advertising to communicate that it is the largest shopping center in its market and has 65 stores unique to northern Nevada. Creative approaches included an "in the bag" concept that used key mall stores' shopping bags and a new signature look using a colorful design and illustrated shopping bag.

Ads were targeted primarily to the tourist market, but also reached local and rural markets to maximize cost-effectiveness. Vehicles included outdoor ads, airport transparencies, an ad and gift offer in the visitor book placed in hotel rooms, and design of two city buses.

The thrust of the promotion was to get Meadowood brochures, coupons, and gift-with-purchase offers into as many visitors' hands as possible. A visitor survey program at the mall's customer information center would monitor the sources and demographics of tourists who visit the mall and redeem incentives.

The team also built on its relationship with the convention and visitors authority (RSCVA) to cross-market to visitors, conventioneers, and attendees of special events.

For example, the team created 40,000 shopping bags, each filled with a mall brochure and gift-with-purchase offer, which RSCVA distributed to conventioneers. RSCVA also sends Meadowood information-packets to convention planners, operates an in-mall visitor service center, and represents the mall in its sales mission.

The gift-with-purchase offer was made in three ways. Visitors who had made a purchase would receive a free canvas tote bag by showing hotel keys (as advertised in the hotel-room visitor book); airline tickets (as advertised in in-flight magazines); or the coupons placed in the convention bags. Cost of the tote bags was offset by a bank's sponsorship.

The center team also developed a three-pronged referral program, which included coupon cards given to all deplaning passengers traveling on Reno Air, and marketing packets distributed to airline ticket wholesalers and travel agencies. The third component was a key card, distributed by hotel personnel, that could be redeemed at the mall for a coupon book. A 10-minute long-distance calling card was offered as an incentive to redeem the coupons; it was financed with a sponsorship by a hotel-casino.

The final step was to improve brochure-rack service, so that a total of 60,000 Meadowood brochures would be distributed annually from more than 200 racks throughout the market.

Results

For the period December through April, monthly sales increased an average of 26% over the prior year. Visitors showed hotel keys, airline tickets, and coupons from their convention bags to redeem 11,561 gift-with-purchase canvas tote bags between December and May. Surveys of those redeeming gift-with-purchase offers showed that 57% of the respondents had never visited the center before.

The convention bureau distributed 4,059 Meadowood convention packets from December through April; hotel personnel distributed 1,951 key cards for coupon books from January through May; and 34,347 people visited the in-mall visitor center from December through May.

EXPENSES

Creative	$ 2,390
Convention package	29,745
Convention planner packets	1,000
Ticket wholesaler packets	1,000
Outdoor ad	36,300
Airport transparencies	25,430
Visitor publication ad	25,000
Bus sides	50,000
In-flight magazine ad	4,000
Key card/coupon book	6,805
Bus shuttle card	1,350
Canvas bags	15,000
In-mall visitor center signage/support	1,000
Customer info center signage/amenities	1,270
Brochures/rack-service fees	7,300
Surveys	1,500
Total	$209,090

Credit

Owned and managed by: The Taubman Co.
Professional recognition to:
Stephanie Kruse, president, Kruse & Parker Advertising; Cynthia Moore, center marketing director; Sheila Armstrong, regional marketing director; Denise Anton-David, senior vice president, marketing.

—from *Shopping Centers Today*
1996 Maxi issue

- Direct mail is best used for domestic rather than international tourists. Mailings to organizations and individuals in certain postal code areas or demographic profiles can generate tourist visits. Sources for names of potential recipients include:

  - Data captured from your center's own shoppers through surveys, membership in a Preferred Visitor Program, or filling out of personal information cards for coupon redemption
  - Lists obtained from your local tourist bureau of out-of-towners (individuals or groups) who have inquired about tourist activities and sights in the area
  - The target area's CVB, which may be able to furnish lists of prospective visitors from its own area
  - Local convention bureau information regarding contacts for convention groups or individual convention attendees.

What to Include in Ads

In addition to the mall's "branded" advertising message, center advertisements and direct mail materials could include these items:

- A clear indication of the center's location, with area map for finding it
- A map of center retailers and services
- A list of merchants
- A directory of mall retailers
- A list of center amenities for visitors, such as currency exchange, no sales tax, or public transportation connections
- Pictorial material (photo or other artwork)
- A toll-free telephone number to call from the home state or from countries of important tourist groups—for inquiries about the center, its hours and location, possible tours, and so on
- Information about upcoming special events at the mall or stores.

Websites

The Internet is a cost-effective means of reaching a distant shopping public. Travelers increasingly use Internet resources in planning their trips. Some of the ways in which shopping centers can tap into this new advertising medium are to:

- Create an attractive website with the same message and center information as your shopping center brochure. List your website with the major search engines. Include these items on your website:

  - Links from your website to the sites of other local tourist attractions and travel-related organizations, such as the Chamber of Commerce or visitors bureau (and request return links from theirs to yours).

- Instructions for contacting the center by phone, fax or e-mail. In seeking interaction, limit web offerings to what you can handle effectively.
- A special section for out-of-town guests, listing services for tourists such as center amenities and group shopping package information.

- Mention the website and e-mail address in promotional materials and ads.
- Use your e-mail connection or an interactive web page as a market research vehicle to seek out personal information about tourist shoppers, such as their names, telephone numbers and e-mail addresses, in exchange for an incentive.
- Consider setting up a home-shopping capability through the website if you have the capability to respond to orders in a timely manner. This means allotting personnel to handle merchandise orders and having adequate inventory to fill them.

The quality of the website, like other advertisements, will reflect on the mall's image. Ensure that someone is specifically delegated to the task of keeping the site current.

Evaluating Your Advertising

Self-tracking is crucial in order to know which advertisements are achieving good results for your center. For effective self-tracking, you should:

- Have a defined target audience and a clear goal for all advertising initiatives. A typical objective might be to increase overall tourist traffic (or visits by a particular tourist group) by 10 percent in one year; exit surveys or responses to a promotional campaign could provide an estimate of actual growth.
- Whenever feasible, include some means of tracking an ad's effectiveness. This could be a discount coupon or a voucher for a gift, or a special telephone number included only in certain direct mailings. Record the number of responses on an ongoing basis.
- Recognize the limitations of any tracking system. The number of coupons redeemed won't reveal the sales generated by a campaign, for example. The cumulative effect of advertising is also not quantifiable; marketing is a long-term process requiring time to develop patronage for the center.

Be observant of other local attractions and businesses that cater to tourists, such as local restaurants, retail stores and service businesses; competing malls; hotels; area cultural sites and other leisure attractions. Regularly monitor your competitors' advertising in media designed to reach visitors, and compare your center's advertising performance to see how you measure up.

4

Special Events

Special events oriented to tourists offer several benefits. They can add value to a traveler's visit; raise the profile of the shopping center and provide an opportunity for positive media coverage; establish or strengthen the image of the center as an entertaining, "fun" destination; and associate the center with a charitable cause or with celebrities and dignitaries who have positive publicity value.

Identifying Events for Tourists

Tourists appreciate many of the same special events that local shoppers enjoy. Appropriate events for the tourist visitor could include:

- Fashion shows with celebrity models
- A spring flower and garden show
- An ethnic festival with cultural displays and activities
- An Easter parade of customers' outfits with prizes to those wearing the best hats
- A charity costume ball
- Clowns, jugglers and musicians performing in center court
- After-hours sales or other discount-related promotions
- Walking tours of the mall or of an adjacent historic or scenic area
- Contests or competitions with giveaways and prizes.

While a wide range of events may draw tourists to the mall or lengthen their stay, the following types seem to have particular appeal for an out-of-town or foreign visitor:

- Events with a local character or a regional focus. Many tourists travel in order to gain firsthand experience of a different geographic area or

39

culture. Domestic and foreign visitors alike will respond positively to a local artisans' fair, an exhibition relating to regional cuisine or history, or a community Homestead Days celebration.

- Events with a link to home. A cultural exposition showcasing an international tourist's home country or a visiting celebrity from that country can capture a foreign visitor's attention.
- Events that are distinctly American. For international travelers in particular, occasions with a U.S. or North American character will have an exotic interest. These might include: seasonal observances or holiday celebrations; sports events or competitions; events with a cultural or historic focus; celebrity guest appearances and performances.

Ensure that special events acquaint tourists with the center. Take steps so they will be attracted to stay and shop before or during the event:

- Feature merchandise from center retailers in the event, such as apparel in a fashion show, and identify its origin.
- Tie the event to mall retail or entertainment venues, for instance, offering a free children's cartoon afternoon in the mall cinema multiplex.
- Include giveaways and prizes of merchandise donated by merchants, with acknowledgment of the donor retailer.

Planning

Special events for tourists should support and complement the strategies and objectives of the center's tourist marketing program. To accomplish that, a center might do the following:

- Target a key tourist market group or profile
- Time events to coincide with a slow sales period that might be improved or to capitalize on a peak tourist season
- Involve and show hospitality to key tourism contacts such as concierges, travel agencies and the media
- Provide positive publicity for the center to the tourism and consumer markets.

Special events should have a target market, a goal or goals and a budget. They might seek to:

- Raise awareness of the center with a particular tourist market
- Increase tourist traffic (or traffic from a particular tourist market segment) over a particular period
- Increase center sales during a certain time period
- Attract significant media coverage of the event and the center
- Raise funds for a charitable cause
- Introduce new retailers or mall features, such as a new entertainment tenant, to the market.

Creating Partnerships

Consider approaching the following potential partners to assist in an event with publicity, materials, staff or money:

- The local CVB or other community tourism agency
- Your center's partners from the tourism/travel industry
- Community and regional businesses
- Community groups whose activities relate to the kind of event you are planning
- International guests and celebrities
- Retailers in the center.

Offer partner organizations or businesses something in return for assistance, such as co-promotion with their logo, a kiosk at the event with their own publicity, or complimentary tickets to functions connected with the event.

Marketing management may consider hosting an event outside the center's local trade area in order to raise the shopping center's profile in a particular market. To maximize impact:

- Choose an event relating to the center's retail merchandise, such as a fashion show.
- Invite local businesspeople, media, dignitaries and celebrities to attend, possibly offering them a pre-event reception or meal.
- Give attendees vouchers to present when they travel to the area and visit your center.
- Allocate part or all of the proceeds from the event to benefit a charity in the target area.

For overseas and other distant markets, it may be more cost-effective to organize the event in conjunction with a visit as part of other tourist marketing activities, such as participation in a trade mission or travel trade show in the area.

A charitable benefit event can bring in additional partners. Fund-raising might benefit a particular tourist country or locality, for instance, with a disaster relief campaign. Solicit co-sponsorship from companies such as airlines that serve that area, or from community groups with an interest in or link to the charity.

Besides generating goodwill, a charity event may be relatively low-cost for a center if sponsors partly or largely cover expenses.

Promoting

Communications to tourist feeder markets should be scheduled well before the event, at a time when potential visitors are making plans for travel—as much as a year in advance in some cases. Pre-event publicity could include:

- Releases to local tourist and travel agencies that market travel outside the area
- Ads and mailings (or e-mail releases) to travel industry contacts in the target market area
- Direct mail announcements to previous shoppers in the target market
- Media advertisements in feeder market consumer publications and broadcast media
- Package incentive offers based around the event, such as discounted hotel rooms and airfares for tourists around the date(s) of the event or motorcoach tour specials with free meals for drivers and discounts for passengers.

Local consumer advertising can be timed closer to the date of the event, to inform tourists who have already arrived in your center's vicinity. Include announcements of upcoming special events on the center's voice mail recording.

Evaluating

Track special events in terms of how well they achieve their goals. Measure response from tourists by:

- Counts of bus visits
- Counts out-of-state cars in parking lots
- Responses to tourist programs such as tax rebate applications or visitor center inquiries during the event
- Sales of tourist-specific merchandise during the event
- Coupon redemptions by non-locals.

After capturing this information, add it to other center research findings to use for future market planning.

5

Merchandise Mix

There is no single "right" merchandising approach for all tourists, because tourist needs and interests vary widely. Like other visitors to the mall, tourists shop for three main reasons:

- For necessary items
- For a wide selection of merchandise and services at a favorable price level, consistent with quality
- For leisure and entertainment on a trip; for stimulation, relaxation and amusement.

Tourists differ in their rationale for shopping. Some groups may visit with only one of these objectives, while others are motivated by all three. Knowing who your tourists are can provide clues as to the type of merchandise mix that will work best for this market. Consult center market research and talk with tenants to determine the following:

- What is motivating tourist shoppers to make a visit to your center? Which of the above three shopping motivations is dominant?
- Which stores are frequented most by visitors from outside the center's local trade area?
- What types of merchandise are purchased most frequently at your shopping center by tourists (and at what price points)?

While customer habits vary widely, many tourists share certain broad general patterns of shopping behavior. Ask whether the following tendencies are typical of tourists visiting your center:

- A large proportion of tourists are on vacation, a time when they have more time to shop than during their weeknights and weekends. With more time, they will likely allow themselves to spend more than at home. Impulse purchases—items that the shopper did not specifically come to the mall to find—are a natural result of this situation.

- Tourists visit the area and the mall as part of a travel experience, and may wish to take away a tangible reminder of that occasion. Gifts for those not along on the trip are also a high-priority category on many tourist shopping lists.

Department Stores

Department stores are often favorite destinations of tourists for many reasons, including:

- Depth of merchandise selection. Many tourists come to buy certain items in quantity or to purchase for friends and family members at home as well as themselves.
- Breadth of merchandise inventory. Visitors can do one-stop shopping and seek out items that cannot be purchased at home.
- Ease of locating and viewing merchandise without customer service assistance. For international visitors with a language problem, the open format of department store space permits easy self-help and locating of appropriate merchandise visually.
- Price point. Department stores usually offer merchandise at different price points, including the middle-range pricing preferred by many tourist customers.

International, National and Local Retailers

A successful mall merchandising plan will take into account the shopping habits and preferences of tourists who visit the center, and ensure that popular merchandise categories are well covered. An appealing combination of stores for tourists will include retailers who are familiar to them along with novel store names. A mix of three types of stores may work well:

- International retailers for the power and credibility they bring to the center. Well-known leading brands are a draw for shoppers in different price points. Status-brand, upscale shoppers are attracted by merchants with exclusive or high-fashion lines of merchandise.
- National retailers for their cultural character. Foreign visitors come to the United States to shop because they want American-style shopping, with American stores and brands. Most international tourists are not seeking the same merchandise mix or retail store complement available at home.
- Local retailers for local color and uniqueness. Many people travel for the experience of another culture, including a different shopping culture. Consequently, stores that seem to be "for tourists only" are not widely appealing to them; visitors like to shop where locals shop. (An exception is the outlet selling local souvenirs.)

The Forum Shops
At Caesars

The Forum Shops in Las Vegas created a billboard on the main thoroughfare for McCarran International Airport. The billboard serves as a strong visual presence seen by 35,000 locals and more than 30 million tourists yearly. (Shopping bags have replaced the oars on the Roman galley ship featured on the billboard.)

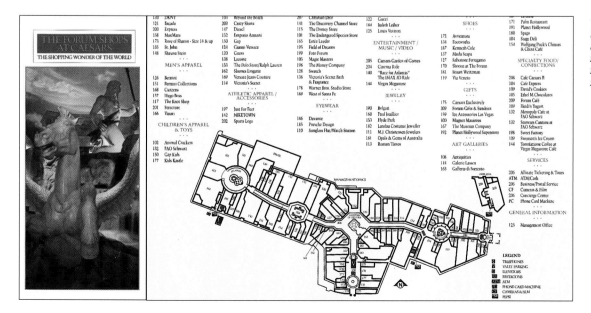

The tenant mix in the brochure for The Forum Shops includes retail names that are recognized by international tourists.

130 DKNY	103 Beyond the Beach	207 Christian Dior	122 Gucci	171 Palm Restaurant
121 Escada	203 Crazy Shirts	141 The Discovery Channel Store	184 Judith Leiber	**SHOES**
200 Express	147 Diesel	115 The Disney Store	125 Louis Vuitton	191 Planet Hollywood
158 MaxMara	152 Emporio Armani	101 The Endangered Species Store		180 Spago
173 Rose of Sharon - Size 14 & up	150 Gap	165 Estée Lauder	**ENTERTAINMENT /**	173 Avventura	104 Stage Deli
135 St. John	134 Gianni Versace	195 Field of Dreams	**MUSIC / VIDEO**	134 Footworks	154 Wolfgang Puck's Chinois & China Café
148 Shauna Stein	120 Guess	199 Foto Forum		187 Kenneth Cole	
	138 Lacoste	105 Magic Masters	205 Caesars Garden of Games	137 Moda Scarpa	**SPECIALTY FOOD/**
MEN'S APPAREL	133 The Polo Store/Ralph Lauren	196 The Money Company	204 Cinema Ride	127 Salvatore Ferragamo	**CONFECTIONS**
	162 Sloanes Lingerie	128 Swatch	140 "Race for Atlantis"	170 Shooze at The Forum	208 Café Caesars II
126 Bernini	169 Versace Jeans Couture	136 Victoria's Secret Bath & Fragrance	The IMAX 3D Ride	181 Stuart Weitzman	204 Café Express
151 Bernini Collections	114 Victoria's Secret	178 Warner Bros. Studio Store	144 Virgin Megastore	119 Via Veneto	109 David's Cookies
168 Cutzens		189 West of Santa Fe			105 Ethel M Chocolates
157 Hugo Boss	**ATHLETIC APPAREL /**		**JEWELRY**	**GIFTS**	209 Forum Café
117 The Knot Shop	**ACCESSORIES**	**EYEWEAR**		175 Caesars Exclusively	109 Heidi's Yogurt
201 Structure			190 Bvlgari	209 Forum Gifts & Sundries	132 Monopoly Cafe at FAO Schwarz
166 Vasari	197 Just For Feet	186 Davante	160 Fred Joaillier	159 Ice Accessories Las Vegas	
	142 NIKETOWN	185 Porsche Design	153 Hyde Park	102 Magnet Maximus	132 Stairways Cantina at FAO Schwarz
CHILDREN'S APPAREL	202 Sports Logo	110 Sunglass Hut/Watch Station	182 Landau Costume Jeweller	167 The Museum Company	198 Sweet Factory
& TOYS			111 M.J. Christensen Jewelers	192 Planet Hollywood Superstore	109 Swensen's Ice Cream
			161 Opals & Gems of Australia		144 Torrefazione Coffee at Virgin Megastore Café
102 Animal Crackers			113 Roman Times	**ART GALLERIES**	
132 FAO Schwarz					**SERVICES**
150 Gap Kids				108 Antiquities	
177 Kids Kastle				118 Galerie Lassen	205 Allstate Ticketing & Tours
				163 Galleria di Sorrento	ATM ATM/Cash
					206 Business/Postal Service
					CF Cameras & Film
					206 Concierge Center
					PC Phone Card Machine
					GENERAL INFORMATION
					123 Management Office

LEGEND
- TELEPHONES
- VALET PARKING
- ELEVATORS
- RESTROOMS
- ATM
- PHONE CARD MACHINE
- CAMERAS & FILM
- PEPSI

Franklin Mills

Tourism plays a vital role in the marketing mix that has made Franklin Mills, a value-oriented shopping center in Pennsylvania, into a successful shopping and entertainment center, drawing more than 19 million visitors in 1998 through its domestic and international tourism programs.

The Franklin Mills Coupon Book offers shoppers discount coupons, welcomes non-English–speaking tourists in several languages and features local attractions of interest.

The Franklin Mills Directory informs shoppers about the center's merchandise mix, store locations and travel and tourism incentives, among other areas of interest.

Alliances with transportation companies are helpful in tourism-oriented programs where tourists without cars need transportation between the hotel and the shopping center.

Mall of America

In all, 40% of the Mall of America's 42 million annual visitors are tourists, defined as shoppers who live beyond a 150-mile radius from the center, which is located in Bloomington, Minnesota.

The Mall of America Coupon Book gives tourists store discounts, informs them about partnerships with local hotels and alerts them to city tourist attractions.

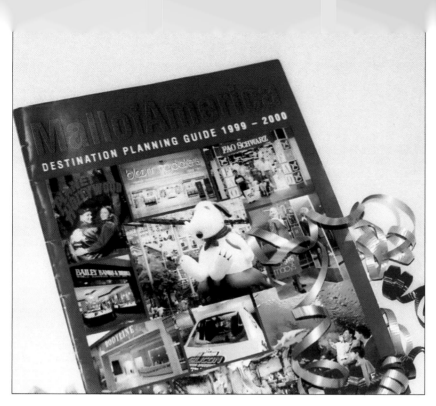

The Mall of America Destination Planning Guide includes a section on tourism services, which provides information on group tours.

The combination of retail and entertainment is a potent draw for the Mall of America, whose numerous attractions include Camp Snoopy's Amusement Park.

CAMP SNOOPY

A spiraling rollercoaster and the bright lights of a Ferris wheel welcome visitors to Mall of America's famous centerpiece, Camp Snoopy, the largest indoor family theme park in the nation.

More than twenty-five remarkable rides and adventures shape the seven-acre park, which also features eight mouth-watering places to eat, plenty of entertainment, and of course, shopping! Kids will love appearances by the Peanuts Gang—Linus, Lucy, Charlie Brown, and that lovable Snoopy!

Ride Highlights

Paul Bunyan's NSP Log Chute — an exciting water adventure ride in a hollowed-out log, ending in a 40-foot plunge over a waterfall.

Pepsi-Ripsaw Rollercoaster — a breathtaking chase above treetops and around the park.

Skyscraper Ferris Wheel — get a bird's-eye view of Camp Snoopy from this giant 74-foot Ferris Wheel.

The Mighty Axe — get turned upside-down in this new thrill ride.

Mystery Mine Ride — become part of the action in a simulated real-life movie adventure.

www.mallofamerica.com

Admission to the park is free, just pay per ride or attraction. Enjoy Camp Snoopy rides all day with an Unlimited Ride Wristband for $19.95.

Check-out Camp Snoopy's new attractions coming spring 1999: Frog Hopper ride, Ghost Blasters, an interactive dark ride and a 25 ft. Climbing Wall.

Take a break from the rides at any of the 8 restaurants including:

* Stampede Steakhouse
* Stadium Club Sports Bar and Grill
* Burger Zone Express
* Betty Crocker Kitchen
* Kemps Ice Cream Cafe

Special Events

Call (612-883-8600) or check our website at www.mallofamerica.com to receive more information on what's planned for these fun-filled family events:

April	Easter
May	Mother's Day
June	Father's Day
October	Camp Spooky
November	Camp Santa — Santa and Holiday Festivities
December	New Year's Eve

612-883-8600

PIER 39

Market research confirms that tourists comprise 60%–70% of PIER 39's customer mix, depending on the season. The remaining 30%–40% are locals, who provide visitors known as VFRs—"visiting friends and relatives."

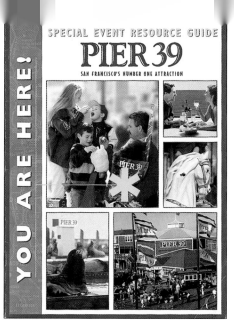

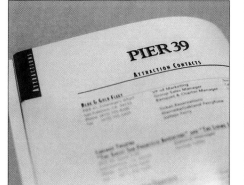

The PIER 39 Special Event Resource Guide gives visitors information on all of the restaurants and attractions at the center.

San Francisco's PIER 39 is highly successful as a tourist attraction, with an advantageous location on the waterfront adjacent to the popular Fisherman's Wharf.

Resort Tourism

A resort area, such as this one in Canada's Whistler, British Columbia, supplies a captive market of tourists, an advantage that can make resort areas highly successful retail venues.

Desert Hills Premium Outlets

Desert Hills Premium Outlets in Cabazon, California, provides multilingual greeting signs, multilingual audio greetings, international sizing charts and an English- and Japanese-speaking concierge and directory, among other amenities created especially for international visitors.

Specialty Short-Term Retailers

Specialty short-term retailers can be useful in achieving a merchandise mix that is well suited to the center's particular tourist market. Center merchandising managers can use these tenants to:

- Extend or broaden the center's merchandise offerings
- Fill gaps in the merchandise mix
- Add seasonal merchandise.

Kiosks, carts and vendors offer advantages to centers that merchandise for tourists, such as:

- A low-risk means of testing visitor demand for new types of merchandise on a short-term basis
- The ability to offer popular impulse purchases such as souvenirs and mementos or refreshments that may not be part of the in-line merchandise mix
- Location of merchandise in high-visibility common area locations and high-traffic areas in the mall (such as near entrances where most visitors will pass), which encourages impulse spending
- Flexibility in merchandising to reflect different tourist travel seasons.

Entertainment

Entertainment is an important enhancement of retail offerings in marketing to tourists. Including entertainment elements in the mall and in the tenant mix can increase the center's attractiveness to tourists, since it will:

- Strengthen the center's appeal as a tourist destination
- Extend shoppers' time in the center, with a resulting increase in sales
- Differentiate the mall from other shopping centers
- Create a more pleasant and/or exciting shopping experience
- Encourage repeat visits and word-of-mouth referrals to other tourists.

Many types of mall features and facilities can offer entertainment to the shopper, such as:

- Center-owned features—a children's play area, carousels, amusement rides or skating rink, and so on
- Retailers that offer an innovative, exciting shopping experience in their stores, such as book superstores, theme restaurants, stores with merchandise try-out areas or interactive display concepts
- Common area live entertainment: strolling musicians, magic shows, celebrity appearances at center court, Santa's Village, and so on
- Tenants that provide recreational entertainment, such as an amusement park, cinemas, and video arcades

Strategies for Inventory

Tourists can place very different demands on retailer merchandise inventory than local shoppers. Center management can assist merchants in dealing with this difference in several ways. They can, for example, check research and survey information to identify when and how tourists might affect sales patterns in the center. Some questions to consider:

- What major shopping occasions (such as domestic or foreign holidays) and seasons bring high levels of tourist traffic to the center?
- Which merchandise items are popular purchases for tourists?
- Are there special requirements for a particular tourist group, such as a large stock of certain sizes?
- What customized promotions, signage or special amenities might be offered for particular tourist contingents—a Spring Break sale during college vacation, or banners with greetings in Spanish during times of peak visiting by Latin American shoppers?

Where there are different tourist profiles with very different shopping patterns, this information may need to be broken out for each group.

Discuss this type of information regularly with merchants to convey the importance of tailoring merchandise for the tourist and to explain the character of the center's tourist market.

Advise retailers that to prepare for tourist customers they might:

- Adjust inventory levels at times of high tourist traffic to include a larger supply of items that are popular with tourists and a higher proportion of specially sized or other specialized items needed by particular tourist groups
- Display popular items more prominently in the window or storefront
- Offer promotions based around tourist-preferred merchandise
- Hire bilingual staff and prepare signage in different languages for times of peak international tourist traffic
- Be ready with current information tourists may need, such as details on sales tax rebates or duties.

- Colorful and unusual design and decorations in the shopping center
- Mall theming, which can include a retail mix that extends the theme—for example, a shopping center with a waterfront motif might have tenants whose decor and merchandise follow a nautical theme
- Dining opportunities at restaurant and food courts.

In deciding on entertainment elements with tourists in mind, shopping center management should consider these factors:

- The mall's identity. What types of retailers and entertainment programs or fixtures are appropriate to the shopping center's "brand" and image?
- The makeup of the center's customer market. What kind of entertainment would best serve both tourist and local shoppers?

Dining Venues

Food offerings are also part of the total shopping experience, but may need to be adjusted to reflect tourist tastes. Some special considerations might be that:

- Tourist visitors may have a range of food preferences different from the center's core dining market. A wide selection of dining options at the food court and in-line restaurants can maximize sales to the out-of-town visitor.
- Tourists from outside the U.S. often want to try U.S.-style food, but may also appreciate something familiar. To meet this need, centers could include a restaurant or food court unit that serves the national or ethnic foods of leading tourist groups.

Merchandise Mix Evaluations

To get feedback about the merchandise mix, shopping centers can conduct brief customer surveys on customer comment cards, by e-mail or as part of other research. Talking informally with tourists about their shopping experiences can also yield useful responses. The survey should ask:

- What other brands or retail banners would the tourist like to see in the center?
- What other merchandise would the tourist purchase if it were offered in the center?
- Where else does the tourist shop when in the area?

This information can be used:

- By mall management to support a decision about adding new types of tenants or otherwise adjusting the tenant mix (or leaving it as is)

Resort Retailing

Resort areas offer a captive market of tourists—an advantage that can make them highly successful retail venues. Recommendations to capitalize on the shopping potential of visitors to a resort area:

- Design a continuous retail strip, a familiar and seamless format in which tourists feel comfortable.
- Create a built-in market for shopping by combining street-level retail with mixed uses such as hotels, apartments, timeshare or offices either above or adjacent. Bolster this captive market with a "warm bed" policy.
- Enliven public spaces with street entertainment (street musicians, buskers, mimics) and seasonal kiosks or vendor pushcarts to encourage visitors to linger and browse.
- Offer activities and attractions that appeal to all ages, to families and to locals, which collectively generate enormous traffic. These might include:

  - Mini-golf
  - Trapeze center
  - Rock climbing wall
  - Luge track
  - Horse riding
  - Skateboard park
  - BMX track.

- Include retailers from the following categories, taking into consideration the particular character of the resort environment:

  - Food and beverage (restaurants, bars)
  - Lifestyle retail (clothing, unisex, footwear, jewelry)
  - Entertainment/Recreation (cinema, virtual reality)
  - Convenience (food store, drug store)
  - Services (banking, beauty salon).

- Include some national stores as well as local retailers to give price credibility to the overall tenant mix.
- Select tenants with a view to fostering as much year-round business as possible. Balance daytime and nighttime retail activity to maximize sales opportunities.
- Organize a merchants' association and institute a system of funding for common marketing and promotions.

- As supporting evidence when proposing tenant changes to center owners or other decision-makers
- By the center to convince prospective new tenants of potential demand for their merchandise at the center.

Is it worthwhile to adjust the tenant mix for tourists? The answer will depend on the center's overall situation. Tourism contributes a relatively small part of the total customer market and total sales at many shopping centers. Center management must consider all the center's customer market segments—tourist and local—in deciding what types and price levels of retail and service businesses to include in the tenant lineup. There are at least two points to consider in deciding whether to adjust the center merchandise mix:

- Who is your primary customer base? How important are tourists to the center in terms of overall sales?
- How variable or seasonal is tourist traffic to the center? Steady, year-round shopping by visitors might justify merchandising with the tourist in mind, whereas a tourist market that is limited to certain times of year might not.

6

Amenities and Service

Attracting tourists to the center is not the end of the campaign. A welcoming environment and special amenities and services are important. Among the reasons to offer special amenities and services to center visitors are the following:

- To increase visit time and spending in the center
- To create a more positive, enjoyable shopping experience. Shopping centers must compete as attractions for the tourist visitor, so time spent must be as pleasant as possible if the center is to be competitive
- To encourage return visits to the center and build repeat business. Many tourist shoppers make multiple visits to an area over time
- To generate favorable word-of-mouth promotion. Tourists who have had a pleasant shopping visit may influence other tourists to come.

Types of Tourist Amenities

Among the amenities that shopping centers might offer to tourist visitors is a customer information booth, with staff or a greeter who can:

- Welcome tourists to the center
- Give directions to stores
- Offer advice and assistance in finding specific items
- Speak about local attractions and services
- Provide concierge functions, such as helping with theater bookings and dinner reservations
- Give out coupon packs or other center giveaways on presentation of proof of visitor status, such as a coupon from a hotel or tourist brochure.

Other amenities can be added, depending on budget and tourist volumes. Many would benefit local shoppers as well as tourists:

- Adequate restrooms, including infant change spaces
- Convenient parking
- Public areas to relax or sit down in
- Restaurants, cinemas and other venues for amusement and relaxation during an outing to the center
- Living room–like lounges or waiting areas in which to relax
- Free or bargain-priced shuttle service to and from local hotels, the airport or other local transportation hubs
- Storage area or lockers for luggage or shopping bags
- Free parking for selected visitors
- A visitor center in the shopping center offering tours of stores, programs for spouses of convention-goers, tourist welcome receptions, and so on
- A children's play center and/or drop-off baby-sitting or day care
- Delivery of bulky purchases to the car or bus
- Valet parking
- Complimentary use of strollers, wheelchairs or electric-powered convenience vehicles
- A postal outlet supplying postage stamps, postcards and other mailing needs
- Computer terminals providing e-mail access for shoppers
- Accommodation of overnight stays by recreational vehicles (RVs) on the mall parking lot pad.

Amenities such as those listed above should be supported by a pleasant center environment to create a positive shopping occasion. Interior landscaping, high ceilings, dramatic lighting, music and other architectural and decor elements contribute to the quality of the visit.

Polite and thoughtful customer service on the part of store staff is also critical in creating a customer-friendly occasion.

Hospitality for Groups

Encourage bus tours and other group visits by:

- Having a greeter ready to meet bus tours
- Welcoming new arrivals to the center over the intercom, in their own language if possible
- Offering an introduction to the center, or a brief tour
- Providing entertainment with a local flavor for important groups
- Distributing complimentary packages containing small gifts, a center directory and coupons for savings on food and merchandise
- Giving dining discounts for group meetings, meals and celebrations.

Special amenities might be provided to tour bus drivers and group escorts, whose goodwill can influence where tourists shop. Ensure their comfort during visits with:

- Complimentary refreshments or meals
- A well-appointed waiting room with television, reading materials and other diversions
- Discount coupons or vouchers and small gifts at least equivalent in value to those of the tour participants
- Payment of any parking fees.

Centers may wish to tailor amenities for different groups by:

- Providing customized "fam" tours or technical tours for groups with special interests, such as retail-oriented professional groups.
- Handing out coupon/gift bags with different values according to the type of guest or their shopping potential. Basic bags might include a guest greeting, shopping bag, discount coupon book, a gift such as fragrance sample, a coupon and cup for a free drink, and a gift-with-purchase offer for shoppers spending a certain amount at the center. Enhanced packages could add other premiums such as amusement park tickets or meal vouchers.

Special Amenities for the Foreign Tourist

Visitors from other countries often need special consideration because of differences in language and culture. Listed below are some areas requiring attention and ways in which shopping center management might address them.

- Communicate with non-English-speaking tourists by:

  - Handing out translated versions of the center's printed materials (brochures, coupons and other promotional literature, flyers, and so on)
  - Posting a translated version of the center directory or map prominently in the mall concourse area
  - Having bilingual/multilingual center signage or signage with international symbols
  - Stationing bilingual greeters wearing special uniforms at the mall entrance, in mall concourse areas and in stores
  - Having bilingual staff at the mall's information center or booth
  - Communicating with bilingual phrase cards that show often-used sentences and expressions in both languages
  - Having the telephone answering machine and voice mail options in a second language.

- Be attuned to cultural differences by:

  - Identifying and being sensitive to gestures, words and body language that may offend visitors from another country
  - Learning about the cultures, customs and etiquette of tourists' home countries in order to better understand and relate to visitors. Communicate such information to retailers
  - Offering something familiar to the visitor, such as a sample of food from home with a sample of U.S.-style food.

- Provide information to assist in shopping choices, such as:

  - Sizing charts comparing foreign and domestic apparel sizes
  - Tags on merchandise giving equivalent foreign sizes
  - A list of stores that carry specialized merchandise, such as petite apparel sizes suitable for Asian shoppers.

Share information with retailers about peak visiting periods for certain visitor profiles, so that they can order special inventory in adequate quantities to meet demand.

- Facilitate purchasing by international visitors by offering:

  - A currency exchange service in the shopping center
  - Transaction capability for leading overseas credit card programs, such as JCB, the largest Japanese credit card—this may encourage larger total purchases than might occur with traveler's checks or cash
  - Details about taxes and duties for taking merchandise into the shopper's home country
  - Information for visitors about obtaining sales tax rebates for which they may be eligible.

- Assist in the delivery of purchases by:

  - Providing wrapping and shipment service to the customer's home country through stores or the center
  - Absorbing the cost of postage and offering complimentary wrapping for items exceeding a certain purchase price.

After-Visit Services

Follow up with tourists after their return home to encourage return visits and referrals. Here are some approaches that shopping centers have adopted to remind tourists of their shopping experiences:

- Send direct mailings about appropriate center events, promotions and package tours. Capture names and addresses for a visitor databank in exchange for coupon vouchers or other incentives; or offer foreign tourists membership in your center's International Club, entitling them to direct mailings and catalog special offers.

- Set up a computerized shopping capability via e-mail or the Internet.
- Establish a personal shopping service offering gift selection, wrapping and shipping.
- Enable shoppers to access the service by e-mail or telephone.

Getting Retailers Involved in Service

Retailers and their customer service staff are often the main point of direct contact with tourists, so they have an important role in creating a tourist-friendly atmosphere at the center. Merchants can support the tourism marketing plan if they:

- Participate in and co-sponsor "fam" tours and promotional events organized by the shopping center
- Note and record information about tourists and their purchases
- Join in trade mission and trade show delegations
- Offer in-store amenities and events to meet tourist needs.

Center management can help involve retailers in marketing to tourists in a number of ways:

- Ask retailers for their own observations concerning tourists.
- Share information with merchants. Have tourism meetings to communicate important findings from customer surveys and other research, or speak one-on-one with retailers.
- Help stores that do not have a press office or public relations firm to make contact with the media.
- Suggest ways to service out-of-town customers and to obtain profiling information (such as where they come from, how they traveled) for future marketing purposes.
- Finance language and cultural workshops for employees at the center to teach simple etiquette and useful phrases for serving international customers.
- Support promotions and events related to tourism hosted by retailers.

Besides customer service staff, all employees at the shopping center—from maintenance and housekeeping personnel to general manager—should be aware that special marketing efforts are being directed at tourists, and they should understand the importance of the tourist market to the center.

SHOPPING
CENTER
PROFILES

Franklin Mills

Motorcoaches pull up at Franklin Mills, a value-oriented shopping center near Philadelphia, with great frequency—as many as 250 have been received on a single day in the Christmas shopping season. Most motorcoach groups have preregistered their

anticipated date and time of arrival with our tourism department, so that a Franklin Mills Greeter will be standing by to welcome them. Upon arrival, a Greeter boards the motorcoach and offers passengers a few words of welcome, mentions any new developments at the mall such as recent tenant additions, and gives pointers about special shopping opportunities or restaurants for a meal break. (For example, "We have a newly renovated food court you may want to visit" or "There's a new Rainforest Cafe. Go and see it if you have time.")

For first-time visitors, a general orientation is given. Retailers receive a monthly schedule of motorcoach tours so they are aware of the number of people expected. This allows them to staff and stock inventory accordingly. The center is prepared for unexpected motorcoach groups as well.

The security staff directs incoming buses to a designated welcome area at one of several entrances to the center. The motorcoach driver is instructed where to park and invited to use the motorcoach drivers' lounge—a room with reclining chairs, tables, TV and restroom. Passengers are told where their motorcoach will be parked when they return.

As they step down from the bus, the Greeter gives each tour participant a coupon book and complimentary shopping bag. The tourists enter the mall and disperse to explore the many retail venues inside.

The tour group leader signs in the group, which provides a name and address for future marketing purposes. The group leader and motorcoach driver each receive a coupon book and shopping bag, plus a gift certificate or voucher for a free meal.

Special events at the center and the attendant publicity also help to raise the mall's profile. To attract tourists, for example, performances of excerpts from *The Nutcracker* have been given in the central court during the Christmas season.

The local tourism bureau has been active in setting up cooperative alliances and package deals involving hotels, attractions and shopping, and Franklin Mills participates in many of these.

The mall has developed partnerships with local hotels through joint promotions and special package offers marketed by the hotel(s) and tour operators. Hotel guests who present a room key from a participating hotel at the shopping center information kiosk are given an incentive such as a coupon book and shopping bag. Hotels capitalize on this market by offering special two-night shopping packages and, in turn, furnish information to the center about tourist groups and conventions that are coming to the area. Tourists booking these package tours fill many local hotels for the weekends on which the promotion is offered. A similar arrangement is made for patrons of selected area car rental companies.

Co-op advertising with other local attractions such as Sesame Place in nearby Bucks County has been effective as well. Casinos and gambling are the biggest single market draw for motorcoach visits to the area, so the center uses this connection as another extension of its own marketing campaign. Complimentary tickets for shows at the casino are given out to selected shoppers, and the casinos in turn promote the center to motorcoach tours with distribution of coupon books or other incentives. Franklin Mills occasionally teams up with a casino for a special show, which generates media publicity.

A Franklin Mills marketing venture is "Shop Pennsylvania," a campaign partially subsidized by the State to attract tourists to tax-free shopping. Over seventy participants, including shopping centers, boutiques, hotels, restaurants, attractions and transportation companies have joined together in this promotion.

Franklin Mills works closely with our CVB and State Office of Tourism to help defray some of the trade show expenses. We make full use of our affiliation with our CVB and the State to promote tourism to the City of Philadelphia and Pennsylvania. Collateral has been produced to support this effort, along with attendance at industry

shows. We have been a driving force within our CVB to bring "shopping" to their attention as an important part of the tourist itinerary.

Franklin Mills has aggressively marketed to the tourism market for over ten years. Initially, our efforts focused on domestic tourism—particularly shoppers who arrive by motorcoach. Almost five years ago, due to the ever-increasing FIT/individual traveler and international market, we expanded our tourism marketing plan to include both of those markets in order to receive a good return on our investment.

Franklin Mills has used a multifaceted advertising plan to reach the domestic and international markets. The center uses a combination of direct mail, print, outdoor advertising and—on a limited basis—radio. Franklin Mills actively works with all the local attractions, destinations, hotels, the CVB and the State Division of Tourism. Attendance at numerous domestic and international trade shows to build relationships is critical to the success of our tourism programs.

Alliances with transportation companies are also productive as a marketing method. Amtrak, Philadelphia City Tour packages, cultural attractions and local restaurants include Franklin Mills in their tourism-oriented promotions.

Direct mail campaigns to the consumer are organized in part by capturing personal information (name, address and perhaps additional demographic data) from the center's own base of previous customers. Franklin Mills uses research into its own shopper pool to identify higher-spending shopper groups such as conventions and international tourists. Inquiries and correspondence from the local or State tourism office can furnish additional leads. Franklin Mills also purchases mailing lists for specific market profiles on ready-to-use labels from the local tourism bureau; these may include names of respondents to a previous marketing campaign or another high-potential market group, such as seniors' groups or church groups. Members of the tourism trades (such as members of the American Bus Association, a motorcoach drivers' organization) can also
be targeted in this way. While expensive, this approach has the advantage of pinpointing a high-yielding market segment.

Attendance at annual trade shows such as the Pennsylvania Bus Association convention is another useful tactic. In addition to motorcoach companies, the show includes many tour group leaders, some of whom are tour operators as well. Fostering ongoing relationships with these professionals is a further method of building the tourism business. Group leaders and bus drivers are treated to occasional celebrity lunches as a gesture of appreciation for their assistance to the center.

The international tourist market is increasingly coming to Franklin Mills, and the marketing team takes part in trade shows and sales missions with U.S. Airways to promote the center to top tour operators overseas. The mall has produced its brochures and coupon books in different languages, and has some bilingual staff members to assist foreign-market shoppers.

Whatever the advertising medium, Franklin Mills endeavors to maintain a constant advertising presence, which is needed for good results with the tourism market.

Franklin Mills remains the leading attraction within the state, with more than 19 million visitors in 1998. Tourism continues to play a vital role in the marketing mix that has developed Franklin Mills into one of the most successful shopping and entertainment centers in the U.S.

Mall of America

The sheer size and range of offerings at Mall of America mean that virtually any type of shopper will find something of interest there. But despite that broad appeal, the Mall has very specific shopper segments in mind in marketing to tourists.

In all, 40% of the Mall's 42 million annual visitors are tourists, defined as shoppers who live beyond a 150-mile radius from the center. The "drive" market beyond that limit consists of day-trippers and others from the surrounding five-state area that commonly arrive by car or bus. A second set of initiatives targets the eleven states outside the "drive" region, and the international market is a third tourist focus.

Cooperative partnerships are a mainstay of the Mall's marketing to each of those three visitor profiles. The Bloomington Convention and Visitors Bureau effectively extends the Mall's marketing efforts by promoting the center to visiting conventions and hotels and in its own literature. Private local businesses are also involved in co-marketing. Theaters promote the combination of a day of shopping with an evening at the theater, for example. Many local attractions such as the zoo, museums and art institute use the proximity of Mall of America as a selling point in their own marketing and promotions. There are thirty-three hotels with 7,500 rooms situated within five miles of Mall of America, all of which offer shuttle service to the center.

As the number one tourist attraction in the state, the Mall is a key marketing site for the State of Minnesota, which maintains a visitor center there to serve tourists and encourage visitation of other parts of the state. The center teams up with the Minnesota Department of Tourism for promotional purposes. A recent collaborative campaign was presented through a thirty-minute infomercial, "Shop 'til You Drop!", highlighting various Minnesota tourist destinations and some of the Mall's shopping and entertainment options. Designed to drive tourism to the state and the shopping center, the infomercial aired in five markets (Milwaukee, Chicago, Des Moines, Las Vegas and Kansas City) over a three-week period, with eighteen placements. While the first three cities represent primary markets for the Mall, the other two (Las Vegas and Kansas City) were second-tier markets that the campaign endeavored to enhance.

Effectiveness was measured via a call to action three times during the half-hour airing, offering an incentive to those who called an "800" number offered in the infomercial. Response was strong—6,582 inquiries came in to the phone line—with a surprisingly large number of calls originating in Las Vegas. The campaign thus achieved its goal of linking up with and extending potential new markets. The Mall broadens the scope of advertising continually to capture new markets, but also works to make secondary markets into primary ones.

The Mall's official airline partner, Northwest Airlines, offers special day-trip shoppers' rates during peak seasons to passengers from destinations across the U.S. Mall of America is situated just five minutes from the Minneapolis/St. Paul International Airport, offering ready access to out-of-state visitors.

In marketing to the international tourist, the Mall participates in both trade shows and sales missions abroad, raising the profile of the center and educating both consumers and tourism agents about it. A main objective is to have travel buyers, tour organizers and travel agents include the Mall in their tour and travel packages for tourists departing from their own countries. Canada, the U.K., Japan, Germany, Switzerland and the Netherlands are important overseas feeder countries for Mall of America tours and visits.

The combination of retailing and entertainment is a potent marketing draw for the Mall of America, whose numerous attractions include Camp Snoopy's Amusement Park, Underwater World Aquarium, Golf Mountain, Lego Imagination Center and NASCAR Silicon Motor Speedway. The shopping/entertainment synergy is especially effective in promoting the Mall to families, whose members often pursue different interests simultaneously during an outing to the center. Family excursions are especially numerous in the summer vacation, back-to-school and winter "cabin fever" seasons. The Mall is also well known for the over 300 celebrity appearances and other special events staged within its doors annually. These occasions are used not only as a marketing vehicles to bring in more consumers, but also as a means of building relationships with media and partners to promote the Mall.

Where merchandising is concerned, the Mall's 520 stores offer an extensive merchandise mix that covers most customer needs and varying price points, from Nordstrom to Old Navy. Shoppers find both familiar retail banners and one-of-a-kind, unique merchants and services. The latter are an important ingredient in marketing to the tourist shopper. Typically, tourists come because Mall of America is a destination, an attraction, and they expect to see something unique. One retail niche especially popular with the tourist is souvenirs, and this merchandise category is covered by the Mall of America Store with logoed merchandise and mementoes.

A Guest Services Area is designated to offer hospitality to all visitors and includes amenities for guests such as a Meet and Greet Service, orientation tours, coupon books, and advice on Mall events or where to find a particular product. The Explore Minnesota Store operated in partnership with the State furnishes information about Minnesota attractions and cultural events and assists with hotel bookings as well.

How does the Mall know whether its marketing efforts are effective? On-mall surveys provide some revealing and useful data, such as the fact that tourists spend twice as much at the center as local shoppers. Tracking through tour operators is another method; counting the number of vouchers for coupon books which are distributed is a simple indicator. Success is gauged not only by the number of visitors but also by the number of tour groups which visit. The Mall pursues innovation in its marketing efforts on an ongoing basis.

The Taubman Company's World Class Shopping

Teaming up with other shopping centers can be a highly effective means of extending your marketing reach.

The pioneer in this approach is The Taubman Company's World Class Shopping, launched in 1995 by five upscale shopping centers to co-promote their retail offerings to the international and domestic traveler. The original members of the program were The Mall at Short Hills, New Jersey; Biltmore Fashion Park in Phoenix, Arizona; Woodfield Shopping Center, Schaumburg, Illinois; Cherry Creek in Denver, Colorado; and Beverly Center, Los Angeles. Their alliance came about at a time when many individual shopping centers were starting to offer tours and programs on a local basis for tourists; the five centers were themselves experiencing growing demand from international tourists and recognized the future growth of that sector. A task force sought to create a common co-promotional affiliation at the corporate level that would market on behalf of all members.

Taubman World Class Shopping quickly developed a strong presence with the travel industry by networking with members and attendance at travel trade shows, beginning with the 1996 World Travel Market convention and the Travel Industry of America PowWow, where the World Class Shopping booth attracted strong media interest as the first corporate delegation from the shopping center sector. At the 1997 PowWow, Taubman World Class Shopping sponsored a Media Relaxation Room for the press—complete with massage chairs—which sparked significant attention. The annual National Tourism Association convention, which brings together motorcoach and other group tour operators, is another important event on the calendar.

A keystone of Taubman World Class Shopping is its creation of benefit packages for tourists in collaboration with business partners. These packages include special amenities, complimentary services, discounted hotel rates and the "Passport to Style," an offer of special discounts and unique offers from merchants and restaurants at the participating centers. World Class Shopping participants may also be offered special rates by other organizations, such as cultural and heritage attractions. Packages vary in price and particular components for different centers.

In 1997, The Taubman Company extended the program to all twenty-eight of its shopping centers in twelve states, and now markets its portfolio of centers as a single brand. The advantages of the collective approach are many: Tour and travel operators can access information about shopping in more than one destination, and the combined branded product captures more attention than any single center can. "It's a win-win situation," said a Taubman spokesperson.

Membership in Taubman World Class Shopping doesn't impinge on individual centers' ability to pursue other partnering possibilities, so they are able to offer shoppers additional benefits as well.

PIER 39

San Francisco's PIER 39 is highly successful as a tourist attraction, with an advantageous location on the waterfront adjacent to popular Fisherman's Wharf. Strong and steady tourist traffic to the city benefits the festival center. Leisure travelers, conventioneers and business visitors flock throughout the year to San Francisco, which continuously ranks as the favorite destination of travelers in many national and international surveys of consumer travel and lifestyle-related publications. The center is keenly aware that its clients need to be pitched on the city as a destination and then pitched on a visit to the center. The tourism industry is San Francisco's largest employer, boasting 60,000 jobs and generating more than $5 billion annually in revenue and taxes for the local economy.

Market research confirms that tourists comprise 60–70% of PIER 39's customer mix, depending on the season. The remaining 30–40% are locals, who provide visitors through what is known as the VFR, or "visiting friends and relatives," market. It is

estimated that more than 3 million people stay in San Francisco hotels each year, while the local market is estimated to provide an additional 16 million visitors. Locals are key to PIER 39's success, because they are employed in various tourism businesses and have great influence concerning the decisions tourists make.

Other reasons for PIER 39's success as a tourist destination are its breathtaking Bay views, fine dining with an emphasis on seafood, quick service restaurants with affordable family pricing, free daily entertainment, fun-filled attractions, a safe, clean and meticulously maintained environment and unique specialty retail.

PIER 39 positions itself as a tourist attraction through a strong tourism marketing campaign. A major share of the center's marketing dollars is allocated to advertising in the city's major tourist publications. Yet like many shopping centers, financial resources and staffing are limited, and marketing staff relies on partnerships to stretch those resources. Ongoing relationships with state and regional convention bureaus and visitors bureaus, airlines, hotels, meeting planners, corporate employee recreation departments and volume leisure travel companies are fostered, and these contacts help to promote PIER 39. Recently, 1,200 key hospitality contacts and their families were invited for a day at the PIER in conjunction with National Tourism

Week, receiving complimentary lunch and VIP attraction tickets. This event was a huge success and will be held annually.

Efficient service and response to the travel industry also help to build collaborative relationships. The Travel Sales Department cultivates personal contacts with travel planners that result in repeat business. The Department also acts as liaison for strategic planning between travel planners and PIER 39's shops, restaurants and attractions. Planners know that they can call on the Travel Sales Department to compile information, put together marketing proposals, customize programs for a particular visitor group, and respond to them quickly and efficiently—all at no charge.

The PIER also participates in various regional sales promotion and public relations programs such as familiarization trips. Meals, complimentary attraction tick-

ets, sales presentations, brochure support or minimal co-op dollars are offered. With the exception of the financial assistance, all of these resources are offered through the travel trade—that is, through tour operators or travel agents. PIER 39's restaurants and attractions benefit from the exposure to these qualified potential clients.

In addition, PIER 39 participates in industry trade shows specifically targeted to San Francisco's major visitor market segments, such as domestic tour companies, international tour companies, meeting and convention organizers and leisure tour companies.

The distribution of PIER 39's Fun Pack, a coupon and brochure packet, is another means of working with hotels, convention and meeting planners, schools and leisure travelers. The packs, which offer substantial discounts and free gifts, are mailed for inclusion in travel documents and are made available at hospitality/registration booths as well as hotel check-in counters. Customized inserts are created for sales promotions and employee recreation programs. Also, PIER 39 has an extremely successful meal voucher program that is tailored to clients on a budget, such as school groups.

To maintain contact with its hospitality industry database, the center distributes a quarterly newsletter communicating what's new. The newsletter provides the center's calendar of events, details of special offers and discounts, PIER 39 fun facts, and profiles of interesting employees and retailers.

Burdines

Miami-based Burdines—The Florida Store, a fashion department store chain, enjoys the advantage of a 100-year history of serving Latin American shoppers, which has brought widespread recognition of the company name in their home countries. But the retailer only recently recognized the need for a concerted effort to target that market.

Burdines staff and management began to realize several years ago that international shoppers were often coming annually or even several times per year to their stores; in other words, these were loyal repeat customers rather than one-time visitors. A tourism program launched five years ago builds repeat business and referrals among members of this shopper segment by trying to create the atmosphere and promotions that appeal to them. Determining what the market likes is less the result of formal surveying than of personal contact with customers—getting to know the people and understand the culture. Management and staff make an effort to get to know who their customers are, the kind of places they like, and the level at which they want to buy. Hispanic tourists vary widely in their shopping habits, and cannot be treated as a single market; every country has its own distinct purchasing patterns and currency variations—even its own holidays—and good customer service involves understanding these facts.

One of Burdines' strengths is the large number of employees who speak Spanish or Portuguese or both. Store decor and interior design have a tropical look which appeals to South Americans, and selection and variety of merchandise are a big selling point: Famous name brands such as Tommy Hilfiger, Calvin Klein and Ralph Lauren are big draws with some Latin American shoppers. Burdines reaches out to Latin American visitors very specifically with special promotions tailored to their holidays and celebrations. Holy Week before Easter is a big time for travel throughout the Latin countries, as is July (the South American winter) for the youth market. One important niche has developed from the Quince or fifteenth-birthday celebrations for Latin American girls, which are often marked by a trip to the U.S. Burdines works with travel wholesalers and operators who specialize in this type of event to offer fashion shows, performances, contests and door prizes for the young women, often scheduled before the store opens. The bridal market is another occasion for trips to shop for attire and home furnishings; a bridal registry program for gifts helps to capture purchases by others for the bridal couple. A highly successful shopping option grew out of the discovery that many passengers from South America arrived in Florida on early morning charter flights, then waited hours until shop-opening time. "Sunrise Shopping" hours extend store operations to let these visitors come to shop early in the morning. Discount programs, with vouchers for coupon book or a "passport to savings," are used extensively in promotions. The success of these marketing efforts can be measured to some degree by the number of international shoppers who carry a Burdines charge card. With forty-eight locations throughout Florida, the company can market itself to travelers visiting any part of the state.

The convention and visitors bureaus of different localities in Florida are important cooperative contacts, and Burdines is featured in their guidebooks for tourists. Burdines representatives participate in overseas sales missions and trade shows around the world, such as the World Travel Mart in London, and work closely with travel agents, wholesalers and operators in Florida and abroad to cultivate tourist markets. The retailer also advertises in some trade magazines for the travel industry, considering that this gives access to tourists before they come to Florida. "You're better to put your effort into the people who are in the business," a company spokesperson says. "Create enthusiasm among the agents and they'll convey that to the tourists." Maintaining personal relationships and having a consistent, ongoing presence have value for establishing relationships in the tourist marketing milieu, he says. "Even going back to the same [trade] show lets them know you're still interested."

Being selective in advertising and show attendance is also part of the Burdines approach. Travel conventions and shows are carefully evaluated to ensure they are appropriate, and staff attends with explicit goals in mind.

The economies of Latin American countries are very fluid, and over the years Burdines has seen many ups and downs in the fortunes of its tourist shoppers from that region. Part of the company's policy with respect to international visitors is to maintain and nurture contacts with their countries of origin even when times are tough and spending is down. Not only do shoppers appreciate this, but their loyalty is maintained until such time as the national financial situation improves, Burdines has found.

Because of rapidly changing world markets, Burdines avoids heavy reliance on one market or even one region, researching and investigating new sources of tourist business constantly. At the moment, Spain, Italy, France, the U. K. and Eastern European countries such as Russia and Czechoslovakia appear to be the next potential targets.

Desert Hills Premium Outlets

The prospect of finding name-brand designer bargains draws both domestic and international visitors to Desert Hills Premium Outlets in Cabazon, California. With 120 high-end outlet stores, this center attracts visitors from nearby Palm Springs as well as visitors to Southern California and Los Angeles. The roster of stores includes top high-profile designers and brands: Donna Karan, Burberry, Coach, Barneys New York Outlet, Ellen Tracy, Giorgio Armani, Guess, Gucci, Kenneth Cole, Lacoste, Max Mara, Nautica, Prada/Miu Miu, St. John, A/X Armani Exchange, Timberland, Escada Company Store, Tommy Hilfiger, TSE, Judith Leiber, Nike and Versace are all represented, among others.

The high-end positioning and presence of well-known brands has proved a magnet to the Japanese tourist, who makes up a significant portion of the international customer base at Desert Hills, while European and Australian visitors also contribute significant numbers.

Making the mall internationally friendly is a top priority. The center has multilingual greeting signs as well as multilingual audio greetings to welcome shoppers. International sizing charts are available, and the English- and Japanese-speaking concierge offers center directories in both those languages. The center information booth is stocked with area information from hotels, restaurants, and attractions to aid the visitor.

The center hosts classes in Japanese culture for retailers and their staff so that they can better understand the etiquette and customs of visitors from Japan and thus offer better customer service. These sessions teach handy expressions in Japanese and promote cultural sensitivity. Instruction recommends specific body language and customs, such as presenting change in a small dish or tray rather than placing it directly in the shopper's hand. Such gestures create a better shopping experience without an awkward ''culture gap,'' and demonstrate that extra care is being taken to welcome Japanese shoppers and make them feel comfortable. This helps to establish a loyalty to the store and the center.

Merchants at Desert Hills understand that a percentage of the store's sales will be from Asian customers and that the store will need to plan accordingly. The mall monitors the time periods when international visits are high, and keeps merchants updated on tourist trends so that they can ready their stock of merchandise and have appropriate sizes in their stores. While Desert Hills has seasonal sales at Memorial Day and Labor Day, seasonality is often determined by the vacation periods and special occasions of its tourism feeder markets, such as Japan's Golden Week in the Spring, which brings large numbers of visitors to the U.S. and to the outlet center.

The center works in close consultation with the Los Angeles Convention and Visitors Bureau, which promotes Desert Hills as a key area shopping destination; it also markets through partnerships with area hotels and other attractions to offer the shopper varied options during a stay in the area. Special combination "Shop and Stay" packages are a successful formula: Desert Hills currently has a Luxury Shopping Package offered in conjunction with local hotels and spas which combines one night's luxury accommodation, a skin care gift, a massage, a continental breakfast and a Desert Hills Premium Outlets VIP Shopper Tote Bag and coupon book. Referrals and word of mouth are regarded as a critical means of building business, whether that referral is from a tour operator, hotel concierge or satisfied shopper recommending the center to a friend.

Chelsea GCA Realty, Inc., Desert Hills' parent company, attends domestic and international trade shows to promote its upscale outlet malls and works to have them integrated within tour operator itineraries for prescheduled tour bookings. Often, shopping centers are included as "optional activities" on preplanned tours.

Desert Hills uses a variety of approaches to identify its customer base: Feedback from merchants, customer intercepts, and international programs with a "bounce-back" mechanism for tracking provide information. Another avenue is consultation with credit card companies, which can assist in analyzing the customer. Information yielded is used for developing a sharper sense of what the shopper wants and for adjusting of the center merchandise mix.

Mall management also make a point of having direct contact with customers to keep in touch with their needs and gauge their reactions to the center. One up-to-date method that works well for overseas markets is regular e-mail correspondence between Desert Hills staff and customers, which is invited by the premiumoutlets.com website. Topics of discussion might range from finding accommodation near the mall to shopping preferences and favorite brands. These dialogues not only are a way of getting to know customers but can also serve to establish and build long-term relationships with them.

The Forum Shops

The average tourist visit to Las Vegas is three days, which means that The Forum Shops faces the challenge of renewing its customer market 10 times per month. On-mall surveys show that 80% of The Forum Shops shoppers are tourists, and one in five of these out-of-towners is an international visitor.

With a dual identity as both shopping center and attraction, The Forum Shops is in competition not merely with other retailers but also with all the other attractions in the area. For this reason, a strong visual presence and effective imagery are crucial in marketing. Las Vegas is one of the most competitive and flamboyant advertising markets in the country, so making an impact calls for something special. The Forum Shops has met this challenge with a new outdoor board designed to resemble a Roman galley ship, with a tongue-in-cheek twist: Instead of rowing oars, the huge board incorporates massive, three-dimensional mechanical arms gripping equally large shopping bags. Logos of seven retail tenants in the Shops are displayed on the bags.

The multimedia board required an elaborate weeklong installation. It measures 62 by 28 feet and is the first of its kind in the U.S. The galley sports a mahogany crow's nest, a specially fabricated PVC sail, seven 60-pound automated fiberglass arms each holding a 3-foot aluminum shopping bag, powered by a custom-designed heavy-duty transmission. Located on the main thoroughfare for McCarran International Airport, the board is seen by 35,000 locals and more than 30 million tourists yearly. It has received national and international publicity, written up in trade publications such as *Outdoor Advertising Magazine*, *Chain Store Age*, and *Shopping Center World*. It also received an Addy Award in Indianapolis, Indiana.

The Forum Shops spends a substantial portion of the total center advertising budget (to which merchants and ownership contribute) on the tourist market. Name recognition is the aim of much of the advertising promotion, and repetition of the center's message is critical, assisted by use of a variety of advertising vehicles. Tourism media such as in-room hotel publications are one effective approach. The Shops are also featured in a multipage section of the hardbound, high-quality publicity published by an independent company and distributed to selected hotels in the area.

Videos at airport baggage carousels and taxi "toppers" (the illuminated panels on taxicab roofs) reinforce the image in the mind of the tourist market. VIP Preferred Customer offerings or other bring-in incentives help The Forum Shops to assess the results of ads.

The Shops make an effort to anticipate amenities that visitors may need, from packaging and local delivery by stores or the concierge to postal service, wheelchairs and strollers. A sign posted at the concierge station lets shoppers know that they can be assisted there with phoning for reservations at shows and restaurants.

The Japanese visitor is particularly important to The Forum Shops, making up more than half of all international customers. Japanese travelers are primarily vacationing, while a lesser number come to Las Vegas for specific conventions and other business-related activities. The Japan Credit Bureau reports that the typical Japanese expenditure at a Forum Shops store is $500.

A relationship with Japan Air Lines (JAL) and its advertising agency, CenteService, has resulted in ongoing campaigns targeting Japanese shoppers. An in-flight video describing The Forum Shops plays during the final twenty minutes of each nonstop Japan-Las Vegas flight, so that travelers who arrive via JAL are aware of the shopping, dining and entertainment features of the center. The Forum Shops and CenteService have designed a program to provide JAL travelers with a "Fun Book" containing a coupon for a drawing at the concierge center. Upon presentation of the coupon, the client draws a ticket from an enclosed container and wins either a Forum Shops designer shopping bag, a $20 gift certificate or a $250 gift certificate. On-mall signage in Japanese makes it easy for the shopper to locate the concierge center and understand the procedure for redeeming the prize.

Most Forum Shops stores employ bilingual sales associates and display promotional signs in Japanese. The management staff has coordinated conversational Japanese classes to assist store personnel in communicating with their Japanese customers. Customer service staff learns simple phrases such as "What size . . . ?" or "What color?" Retailers' inventories include sizes and styles that appeal to the Japanese shopper. Japanese-language brochures are distributed on-mall and to Japanese tour operators. The brochure is also available in seventy brochure racks placed in strategic Japanese outlets in San Francisco, Los Angeles and Las Vegas.

The tenant mix includes a number of international retail names that are recognized as very important to Japanese shoppers, such as Louis Vuitton, Versace, Banana Republic, and Niketown.

The Forum Shops works cooperatively with other tourist-oriented businesses and agencies in the community such as the local chamber of commerce, the news bureau and travel and tour operators. Press relations are important, and the marketing office keeps updated press kits and a good supply of photos on hand for occasions when media are present. There is heavy demand for the center's own "fam" tours and technical tours—at least six a week are scheduled regularly—and tour guides work with interpreters to serve non-English-speaking groups. In addition, there are several group visits per day to The Forum Shops, which are organized by tour operators, and the center provides these tours with updated information and possibly a guide as well.

In the Las Vegas setting, many hotels have their own retail stores and therefore do not furnish shuttle service to other shopping venues. However, hotel concierges are important contacts, and the Shops host events for them to express appreciation for referrals and develop an ongoing relationship. Such appreciation nights might include a meal or refreshments and awards of gifts and prizes. Liaison with the Southern Nevada Hotel Concierge Association is also helpful in maintaining contact.

Market research (by exit surveys, with bilingual intercept personnel for foreign participants) has helped The Forum Shops to define the most important customer groups—for example, that the international customer spends three times as much as a domestic shopper. Shopper demographics and spending are constantly evolving, and research helps to pinpoint trends. In addition to identification of the customer market, The Forum Shops compares its own tourist visitors with the demographics of overall visitors to Las Vegas and follows the shopping habits of local customers. Surveys are conducted every two years to keep tabs on the rapidly changing tourist market.

RESOURCES

This section provides additional resources on marketing to tourists. This is not an exhaustive list, but it is intended to offer helpful suggestions for searching out information on the topic of tourism and shopping.

Reports and Publications

Annual Report. Travel Business Roundtable (New York, 1997).

Employment in the Travel and Tourism Industry by Mandy Rafool and Laura Loyacono. National Council of State Legislatures (Denver, 1997).

Shopping and Cultural/Heritage Tourism: A Special Study of Overseas Travelers to the United States. U.S. Department of Commerce, International Trade Administration, Tourism Industries and The Taubman Co. (Washington, DC: January 1999).

State Tourism Taxes by Mandy Rafool. National Council of State Legislatures (Denver, 1997).

A Report of the Travel and Tourism Industry in the United States. Tourism Works for America (Washington, DC, Reports for 1996, 1997, 1998).

Travel and Tourism: A Legislator's Guide by Mandy Rafool and Laura Loyacona, National Council of State Legislatures (Denver, 1999).

"Travel and Tourism: A Powerful Force for America's Future." Supplement to *The Washington Times*, *The Washington Post* and *USA Today*, April 20, 1994.

Periodicals

Chain Store Age. Lebhar Friedman, 425 Park Avenue, New York, NY 10022.

Shopping Center Business. France Publications, Inc., Two Securities Centre, 3500 Piedmont Road, Suite 415, Atlanta, GA 30305.

Shopping Centers Today. International Council of Shopping Centers, 665 Fifth Avenue, New York, NY 10022-5370.

Shopping Center World. Argus Business, 6151 Powers Ferry Road NW, Atlanta, GA 30339.

Stores. NRF Enterprises Inc., 325 Fifth Street NW, Washington, DC 20004.

Value Retail News. 29399 U.S. Highway 19N, Suite 370, Clearwater, FL 33761.

Articles

"A Cheap New York? For Foreign Visitors, Yes." Tom Redburn. *New York Times*, July 21, 1994.

"A Small Town Faces the Big Malls: Hoping for Just Enough Visitors to Sustain Its Old Charms." George Judson. *New York Times*, June 23, 1996.

"A Survey of Travel and Tourism: Dream Factories." *The Economist*, January 10, 1998.

"America's Hot Tourism Spot: The Outlet Mall." Edwin McDowell. *New York Times*, May 26, 1996.

"Americans Hit the Road with Relish, and Money to Burn." Michael Janofsky. *New York Times*, July 25, 1995.

"Area Luring Tourists to Its Shopping." Suzanne Gordon. *Philadelphia Inquirer*, February 15, 1996.

"A Tale of Two Leaves: Outlet Shopping . . ." Danielle Reed. *Wall Street Journal*, October 17, 1997.

"Bal Harbour's South American Way." Georgia Lee. *Women's Wear Daily*, June 27, 1994.

"Bible Belt's Mecca." Brad Edmondson. *American Demographics*, August 1990.

"Border Outlet Projects Bank on Locals, Thrive on Cross Shoppers." Kris Hundley. *Value Retail News*, February 1995.

"British Malls Target European Tourist." Timothy Harper. *Shopping Centers Today*, May 1996.

"Building a Strong Future for Tourism." A speech by Ed Hogan, founder, owner and chairman, Pleasant Holidays. *Business Wire's Features*, January 27, 1999.

"Bureau Efforts Bring More Tourists, Conventions to City: Annual Report Shows How Bureau Is Selling Houston to Promote City's Economy." Thora Qaddumi. *Houston Business Journal*, September 8, 1997.

"California Balloon Race 1992: Sierra Vista Mall." *Shopping Centers Today* Maxi Awards 1993. International Council of Shopping Centers.

"Castle Rock Outlets Rank High in New Denver Tourism Study." *Value Retail News*, September 1998.

"Centers Reap the Benefits of Catering to Asian Tourists." Sheila Lynch. *Value Retail News*, January 1997.

"Coming to America." Wilbur Zelinsky. *American Demographics*, August 1990.

"Cool Paths of a Hot Summer." Edwin McDowell. *New York Times*, September 2, 1995.

"Courting the Tourist." Anne D'Innocenzio. *Women's Wear Daily*, August 30, 1995.

"Department of Commerce and Taubman Co. Release Results of Cultural Tourism Study: First-Ever Study Examines the Correlation between Travel and Shopping for German Tourists." *Business Wire*, December 30, 1998.

"Discover the World: Seaport Village." *Shopping Centers Today* Maxi Awards 1992. International Council of Shopping Centers.

"Dollar Days for the Cartier Crowd." *Business Week*, August 21, 1995.

"Downtown Gets Malled: Latin American Tourists Are Skipping Downtown Miami for Shopping Trips to Sawgrass and Dadeland." John Fernandez. *South Florida Business Journal*, December 29, 1997.

"Evolution of the MegaProject." Thomas Dunn and Kenneth Prysor-Jones. Supplement to *Urban Land*, March 1995.

"Fewer Foreign Tourists Visiting USA." Cathy Lynn Grossman. *USA Today*, September 20, 1995.

"Fishing for Tourists." *Trendz*, March 1999.

"Florida Basks in Warmth of More Tourists." Martha Brannigan. *Wall Street Journal*, February 20, 1996.

"Florida Tourism Bounces Back." Deborah Sharp. *USA Today*, January 12, 1996.

"Foreign Affairs." Maura K. Ammenheuser. *Shopping Centers Today*, May 1999.

"Foreigners Buy Up New York." David Colman. *New York Times*, April 5, 1998.

"Forget the Beach: Travelers Opt for the Mall Vacations." *Travel Guide News*, July 31, 1998.

"For Them It's a Mall World." Joan Verdon. *The Record*, May 9, 1998.

"Giftus Maximus: Forum Shops at Caesars Las Vegas." *Shopping Centers Today* Maxi Awards 1993. International Council of Shopping Centers.

"Grand Opening: The Forum Shops at Caesars." *Shopping Centers Today* Maxi Awards 1992. International Council of Shopping Centers.

"Hawaii Stores Are Hard Hit by Asia Woes." Laurie MacDonald. *Women's Wear Daily*, April 7, 1998.

"High Prices Cool Summer Travel Forecasts." Jonathan Dahl. *Wall Street Journal*, May 25, 1995.

"Hotel Locations Offer Unique Opportunities for Retailers." Sandra Bailey. *Shopping Center Business*, April 1997.

"In a Universal Quest for Bargains, Japanese Flock to Hudson Valley." Lisa W. Foderaro. *New York Times*, June 18, 1998.

"It's a Mall World After All." Sandra Pesman. *Advertising Age*, December 19, 1994.

"Japanese Skip Waikiki, Head for Kmart." Jim Carlton. *Wall Street Journal*, June 29, 1998.

"Japanese Tourist Courted in American Malls." Paula J. Silbey. *Shopping Centers Today*, February 1991.

"Jumping Through Hoops for Groups." Tom Kirwin. *Value Retail News*, April 1996.

"Lake Buena Vista Caters to Hospitality Workers." Donald Finley. *Value Retail News*, September 1998.

"Leaders Need to Realize Retail and Tourism Gel." Paula Gillingham. *Pacific Business News*, December 1, 1997.

"Luring Foreign Tourists: Mall Officials Realize Importance of International Shoppers." Barbara Hogan. *Shopping Centers Today*, October 1994.

"Malls Look to Focus on Tourist Market." Barbara Hogan. *Shopping Centers Today*, November 1995.

"Money Exchange Cashes in on Opportunity: Convenience Is Currency at Potomac Mills Mall Location That Serves Travelers." Peter A. McKay. *Washington Post*, October 21, 1998.

"Motorcoach Riders Love Outlet Shopping." *Value Retail News*, May 1998.

"New Retailers, Restaurants Boost Indianapolis Tourism Revenue." Courtenay Edelhart. *Responsive Database Services*, May 7, 1997.

"New Tourism Web Site to Ease Cyberspace Journey." Gene Sloan. *USA Today*, March 21, 1995.

"Olla de Oro: Latin American Visitors to U.S. Shopping Centers." Leonard E. Borg Jr. *ICSC Research Quarterly*, Spring 1998.

"Orlando Co-Op Program Targets Latin American Shoppers." Tom Kirwin. *Value Retail News*, December 1998.

"Outlet Centers Fine-Tune Bus Marketing." Dawn Frankfort. *Value Retail News*, December 1990.

"Outlet Centers May Host RVs Overnight." Donald Finley. *Value Retail News*, June 1998.

"Outlet Malls Draw Bargain Hunters." Donna Gable. *USA Today*, November 14, 1991.

"Outlet Malls Draw Tourists to Upstate New York." Kate Walter. *Shopping Centers Today*, January 1990.

"Pack Your Bags: South Park Mall." *Shopping Centers Today* Maxi Awards 1993. International Council of Shopping Centers.

"Public Forum: Reflecting on Tourism Benefits." Patrick Moscaritolo. *Boston Globe*, May 6, 1997.

"Shop Herders: Add Tourist Coordinator to List of Jobs Needed to Keep Malls Running." Suzanne Gordon. *Chicago Tribune*, September 5, 1993.

"Shopping as a Travel Attraction." Suzanne Gordon. *Philadelphia Inquirer*, August 30, 1993.

"Shopping as Recreation Push." June Carolyn Erlick. *HFN*, October 2, 1995.

"Shopping Trips: The Mall Emerges as a Tourist Destination." Molly Brauer. *Detroit Free Press*, September 8, 1997.

"So Far, Games Are a Bust for Atlanta Merchants." *Wall Street Journal*, July 23, 1996.

"South Coast Capitalizes on Tourism." Rosemary Rice McCormick. *Shopping Center Business*, September 1996.

"The Galleria's Tourism Focus—Distinctive Stores, Special Events." Rosemary Rice McCormick. *Shopping Center Business*, May 1997.

"The Outlet as Destination for Those Who Love a Sale." *New York Times*, April 5, 1998.

"Tour and Travel Program: Franklin Mills." *Shopping Centers Today* Maxi Awards 1992. International Council of Shopping Centers.

"The Tourist." Colin Flaherty. *San Diego Magazine*, December 1995.

"There's a Place for Fun in Your Life/Mall of America Grand Opening Gala." *Shopping Centers Today* Maxi Awards 1993. International Council of Shopping Centers.

"Tour Operators Like Personal Touch When Being Courted." Dawn Frankfort. *Value Retail News*, December 1990.

"Tourism Fuels City Economy." Judith Evans and Edward Silverman. *New York Newsday*, April 24, 1995.

"Tourism Grant Helps Mall's Ad Tab: Critics Deem Plan Corporate Welfare." Mary Ellen Podmolik. *Chicago Sun-Times*, February 27, 1995.

"Tourism Industry Unveils Plan to Boost Foreign Visits to US." Elizabeth Ross. *The Christian Science Monitor*, April 3, 1996.

"Tourism Retail News." Randall Shearin. *Shopping Center Business*, January 1999.

"Tourism Sales Promotion." *Shopping Centers Today* Maxi Awards 1996. International Council of Shopping Centers.

"Tourism Vital for New Orleans Center." Heidi Gralla. *Shopping Centers Today*, September 1994.

"Tourist Business Booming at SuperMall." Lynn R. Crosby. *Shopping Centers Today*, January 1996.

"Tourist Destinations' Ugly Word: Outlet Saturation." Gail Walker. *Value Retail News*, July 1992.

"Tourist-Oriented Centers Are a Hit." Paula J. Silbey. *Shopping Centers Today*, May 1993.

"Tourist Programs Hot Ticket for Malls." Faye Brookman. *Shopping Centers Today*, September 1998.

"Tourists Are Sold on Malls: Package Deals Draw Shoppers." Gene Sloan. *USA Today*, December 15, 1995.

"Tourists Turn to Internet for Other Tourists' Tips." Jared Sandberg. *Wall Street Journal*, May 12, 1995.

"Travel Growth to Slow." Cathy Lynn Grossman. *USA Today*, October 17, 1995.

"Vegas Visitors Find Fun Without Games." Robert Macy. *USA Today*, July 27, 1998.

Audiocassettes

All ICSC audiocassettes can be ordered from The Resource Link. Order toll-free at 1-800-241-7785. In Atlanta, call 770-447-0616. For further information, write: The Resource Link, 3139 Campus

Drive, Suite 300, Norcross, GA 30071-1402.
www.the-resource-link.com

"Capitalizing on the Lucrative Tourism Dollar." Chair: Carolyn Feimster. ICSC 1998 Fall Convention. Norcross, GA: The Resource Link.

"Developing a Retail Tourism Program." Chair: Kathy Anderson. ICSC 1999 Fall Convention. Norcross, GA: The Resource Link.

"Developing Tourism Partnerships." Chair: Lalia Rach. ICSC 1999 Fall Convention. Norcross, GA: The Resource Link.

"Developing Tourism Partnerships." Chair: Lalia Rach. ICSC 1999 Spring Convention. Norcross, GA: The Resource Link.

"The Impact of Latin American Visitors on U.S. Shopping Centers." Chair: Leonard Borg. ICSC 1997 Conference. Norcross, GA: The Resource Link.

"Resort and Tourism Projects." Chair: Ian Thomas. ICSC 1999 Spring Convention. Volume I. Norcross, GA: The Resource Link.

Associations

The following is a list of major trade associations that represent members of the tourism and travel industries.

American Bed and Breakfast Association (ABBA), P.O. Box 1387, Midlothian, VA 23113-8387.

American Bus Association (ABA), 1100 New York Avenue, Suite 450, Washington, DC 20005-3934.

American Hotel and Motel Association (AH& MA), 1201 New York Avenue NW, Suite 600, Washington, DC 20005-3931.

American Society of Travel Agents (ASTA), Dept. 0621, Washington, DC 20073-0621 (www.astanet.com).

Association of Destination Management Executives (ADME), 3333 Quebec Street, Suite 4050, Denver, CO 80207-2326.

Association of Meeting Professionals, 1255 23rd Street NW, Washington, DC 20037.

Association of Travel Marketing Executives (ATME), 305 Madison Avenue, Suite 2025, New York, NY 10165.

Council of State Chambers of Commerce (CSC), 132 C Street NW, Suite 330, Washington, DC 20001.

Inter-American Travel Agents Society (ITAS), 450 Meyerland Plaza Mall, Houston, TX 77096-1613.

International Association of Tour Managers— North American Region (IATM-NAR), 65 Charnes Drive, East Haven, CT 06513-1225.

National Association of Business Travel Agents (NABTA), 3255 Wilshire Blvd., Suite 1601, Los Angeles, CA 90010.

National Association of Cruise Only Agencies, 7600 Red Road, Suite 128, Miami, FL 33143.

National Bed-and-Breakfast Association (NB& BA), P.O. Box 332, Norwalk, CT 06852.

National Business Travel Association (NBTA), 1650 King Street, Suite 401, Alexandria, VA 22314.

National Conference of State Legislatures' Travel and Tourism Partners, 1560 Broadway, Suite 700, Denver, CO 80202.

National Council of State Tourism Directors (NCSTD), 1100 New York Avenue NW, No. 450, Washington, DC 20005-3934.

National Tour Association (NTA), 546 E. Main Street, P.O. Box 3071, Lexington, KY 40596-3071.

Tourism Works for America Council, 1100 New York Avenue, Suite 450, Washington, DC 20005.

Travel Business Roundtable, c/o Rush Marburg, 1801 K Street NW, Washington, DC 20006.

Travel Industry Association of America, 1100 New York Avenue, Suite 450, Washington, DC 20005.

Travel Professionals Association (TPA), 216 S. Bungalow Park Avenue, Tampa, FL 33609.

United States Tour Operators Association (USTOA), 342 Madison Avenue, No. 1522, New York, NY 10173.

U.S. Travel Data Center (USTDC), c/o Travel Industry Association of America, 1100 New York Avenue, Suite 450, Washington, DC 20005.

World Travel and Tourism Council, Chaussee de Lahulpe 181, Box 10, 1170 Brussels, Belgium.

U.S. Government

International Trade Administration, U. S. Department of Commerce—Tourism Industries, Room 1860, Washington, DC 20230.